READINGS ON

ONE DAY IN THE LIFE OF IVAN DENISOVICH

OTHER TITLES IN THE GREENHAVEN PRESS LITERARY COMPANION SERIES:

WORLD AUTHORS

Fyodor Dostoyevsky
Homer
Sophocles

WORLD LITERATURE

All Quiet on the Western
  Front
Antigone
Candide
Crime and Punishment
Cry, the Beloved Country
Cyrano de Bergerac
The Diary of a Young Girl
A Doll's House
Medea
Night
One Day in the Life of
  Ivan Denisovich
The Stranger

THE GREENHAVEN PRESS
Literary Companion
TO WORLD LITERATURE

READINGS ON

ONE DAY IN THE LIFE OF IVAN DENISOVICH

Loreta Medina, *Book Editor*

David L. Bender, *Publisher*
Bruno Leone, *Executive Editor*
Bonnie Szumski, *Series Editor*

Greenhaven Press, Inc., San Diego, CA

Every effort has been made to trace the owners of copy-righted material. The articles in this volume may have been edited for content, length, and/or reading level. The titles have been changed to enhance the editorial purpose. Those interested in locating the original source will find the complete citation on the first page of each article.

Library of Congress Cataloging-in-Publication Data

Readings on One day in the life of Ivan Denisovich /
    Loreta Medina, book editor.
        p. cm. — (Greenhaven Press literary companion to
    world literature)
    Includes bibliographical references and index.
    ISBN 0-7377-0563-9 (pbk. : alk. paper) —
ISBN 0-7377-0564-7 (lib. bdg. : alk. paper)
    1. Solzheniëìyn, Aleksandr Isaevich, 1918–Odin
    den§'Ivana Denisovicha. I. Medina, Loreta. II. Series.

PG3488.O4 O368 2001
891.73'44—dc21

                                                        00-057842

> *The writer's ultimate task is to restore the memory of his murdered people.*
>
> —Solzhenitsyn on the role of the writer

Contents

Chapter 1: Themes in *One Day*

1. A Quest for Truth, Justice, and Charity
by Hélène Zamoyska   34

Solzhenitsyn portrays the agonizing living conditions in the prison camp: extreme cold, hunger, hard labor, and tyrannical guards. The author reserves his sympathy for the prisoners and his contempt for the guards and camp administrators as well as Soviet bureaucrats.

2. Moral Choices and Small Victories
by Steven Allaback   42

The author mines the consciousness of Shukhov and finds lessons there for everyone: awareness of one's condition, making choices, relishing small victories, and taking care of one's self while being compassionate to others. Departing from the common picture of Shukhov as a simple, practical man. Allaback portrays him as a complex individual perpetually balancing between preserving his dignity and groveling for crumbs.

3. Work as Redemption *by Olivier Clément*   51

Clément looks at how Ivan Denisovich's act of laying down one brick on top of another to build a wall nourishes his soul. Clément contends that Solzhenitsyn views work as a means of achieving spiritual awareness.

4. *One Day*, a Modern Epic *by Robert Porter*   58

Porter argues that the novel succeeds because of its universality. Shukhov and the other characters are mostly peasants and are semiliterate, which contributes to their credibility. Despite the dehumanizing conformity of their lives, however, the characters retain their individuality.

Chapter 2: The Character of Ivan Denisovich Shukhov

Mir, recounts how Solzhenitsyn's exposé of the prison camp system in Stalinist Russia passed the scrutiny of Communist officialdom: first Nikita Khrushchev and then the Central Committee of the Communist Party.

FOREWORD

*"'Tis the good reader that
makes the good book."*

Ralph Waldo Emerson

The story's bare facts are simple: The captain, an old and scarred seafarer, walks with a peg leg made of whale ivory. He relentlessly drives his crew to hunt the world's oceans for the great white whale that crippled him. After a long search, the ship encounters the whale and a fierce battle ensues. Finally the captain drives his harpoon into the whale, but the harpoon line catches the captain about the neck and drags him to his death.

A simple story, a straightforward plot—yet, since the 1851 publication of Herman Melville's *Moby-Dick*, readers and critics have found many meanings in the struggle between Captain Ahab and the whale. To some, the novel is a cautionary tale that depicts how Ahab's obsession with revenge leads to his insanity and death. Others believe that the whale represents the unknowable secrets of the universe and that Ahab is a tragic hero who dares to challenge fate by attempting to discover this knowledge. Perhaps Melville intended Ahab as a criticism of Americans' tendency to become involved in well-intentioned but irrational causes. Or did Melville model Ahab after himself, letting his fictional character express his anger at what he perceived as a cruel and distant god?

Although literary critics disagree over the meaning of *Moby-Dick*, readers do not need to choose one particular interpretation in order to gain an understanding of Melville's novel. Instead, by examining various analyses, they can gain numerous insights into the issues that lie under the surface of the basic plot. Studying the writings of literary critics can also aid readers in making their own assessments of *Moby-Dick* and other literary works and in developing analytical thinking skills.

The Greenhaven Literary Companion Series was created with these goals in mind. Designed for young adults, this unique anthology series provides an engaging and comprehensive introduction to literary analysis and criticism. The essays included in the Literary Companion Series are chosen for their accessibility to a young adult audience and are expertly edited in consideration of both the reading and comprehension levels of this audience. In addition, each essay is introduced by a concise summation that presents the contributing writer's main themes and insights. Every anthology in the Literary Companion Series contains a varied selection of critical essays that cover a wide time span and express diverse views. Wherever possible, primary sources are represented through excerpts from authors' notebooks, letters, and journals and through contemporary criticism.

Each title in the Literary Companion Series pays careful consideration to the historical context of the particular author or literary work. In-depth biographies and detailed chronologies reveal important aspects of authors' lives and emphasize the historical events and social milieu that influenced their writings. To facilitate further research, every anthology includes primary and secondary source bibliographies of articles and/or books selected for their suitability for young adults. These engaging features make the Greenhaven Literary Companion series ideal for introducing students to literary analysis in the classroom or as a library resource for young adults researching the world's great authors and literature.

Exceptional in its focus on young adults, the Greenhaven Literary Companion Series strives to present literary criticism in a compelling and accessible format. Every title in the series is intended to spark readers' interest in leading American and world authors, to help them broaden their understanding of literature, and to encourage them to formulate their own analyses of the literary works that they read. It is the editors' hope that young adult readers will find these anthologies to be true companions in their study of literature.

INTRODUCTION

Solzhenitsyn believes a writer's duty is to tell the truth. In his acceptance speech for the Nobel Prize in literature in 1970, he said, "It is within the power of writers and artists to . . . defeat the lie." He has made this the cause of his life.

His first major work, *One Day in the Life of Ivan Denisovich*, conceived during long years of imprisonment in a forlorn region of Kazakhstan, marks the beginning of his crusade to tell the truth and resurrect his people's memory. Published in Russia in 1962, the novel describes one day in the life of Shukhov, a simple peasant, and other inmates in a prison camp. Upon publication, the novel was hailed by critics as a major new work in the already rich body of Russian literature.

Critics specifically praised several attributes of the novel: "The very structural principles on which the work is built are remarkable and out of the ordinary," said one reviewer. Another noted, "The imagery, rhythm, and flux of this story are all drawn from the depths of the language of the people." Others were struck by the realism of the novel: "the new sounds . . . are so real and convincing."

While many considered it a fascinating literary work, especially in its use of refreshing language and a double-voiced point of view, many more considered it a political statement—an exposé of the hidden world of concentration camps, and by extension, an indictment of Stalin's rule and the entire Soviet system. Much of the novel's fame today rests on this political content.

THE IMAGE PERSISTS

There are reasons why his political image persists in the mind of the reading public. First, Solzhenitsyn's subject matter—the horror of the prison camps, freedom and its constraints, and the triumph of individual will—easily lends itself to a political reading. Second, Solzhenitsyn went against the traditions of socialist realism by doing away with "optimistic literature" populated by "positive heroes." Instead, he presents an array of complex characters who espouse contrasting but compelling ideologies. Critics and readers see a political message in having no central hero who has a monopoly on truth (which contradicts Joseph Stalin's "cult of personality" and authoritarian rule). Third, Solzhenitsyn wrote during the politically charged time of the Cold War, when the United States and the USSR competed for political and military dominance in much of the world.

Because he came to be seen as opposing so much of what the Soviet Union stood for, Solzhenitsyn became a voice in the wilderness. Although many of his compatriots opposed the suppression of freedom in Russia, his case attracted much more attention in the West. To many in the West, Solzhenitsyn was the lone man fighting a giant.

Still, critics have gone beyond his work's political message. Abraham Rothberg, in *Solzhenitsyn: The Major Novels,* comments on the author's works in general, but the observation rings true for *One Day* as well:

> All of Solzhenitsyn's major works are set in contexts where men have little or no control over their lives—prison, *sharashka* [prison where research is conducted], cancer ward—where human beings are debased and diseased, where fear, tyranny, and pain are endemic and inevitable, but how men live under these circumstances, how they endure and remain men, is Solzhenitsyn's obsession.

POWER IN RESTRAINT

In recent years, with the breakup of the USSR, the gradual democratization of Russia and its former satellites, and the distance offered by time, a more nuanced reading of *One Day,* as well as Solzhenitsyn's other works, has become possible. Author and critic Michael Nicholson comments:

> The power of *One Day* . . . rests not on the absence of the didactic, sermonizing voice, but on its constraint: the verbal and intellectual limitations of Ivan Denisovich and the detailed, quotidian routine of his world are made to contain and enhance the universalizing, and symbolizing impulse that racks the text.

Nicholson adds that in *One Day,* as in Solzhenitsyn's other works, he pursues his engagement with truth through the use of "traditional psychological realism, in which allegorical patterns and moments of lyrical tranquility intimate a universal plane of meaning beyond the grim struggles in the microcosm."

Many believe that *One Day* remains Solzhenitsyn's masterpiece because of its immediacy of language and controlled narrative. Critic George Steiner notes that the novel sharply delineates Russian consciousness in a manner reminiscent of Aleksandr Pushkin and Fyodor Dostoyevsky. He adds that if the twentieth century is indebted to Solzhenitsyn, it lies in his brave acts of preserving mankind's conscience in a "soiled age."

ALEKSANDR SOLZHENITSYN: A BIOGRAPHY

Aleksandr Solzhenitsyn is best known for his monumental works chronicling the atrocities of concentration camp life in the Soviet era. Among other things, he has been called a prophet, a beacon for humanity, and Russia's spiritual father.

Of Solzhenitsyn, Octavio Paz, who won the 1990 Nobel Prize for literature, says,

> If history is the testing ground, Solzhenitsyn has passed the test. His example is not intellectual or political or even, in the current sense of the word, moral. We have to use an even older word, a word that still retains a religious overtone—a hint of death and sacrifice: *witness*. In a century of false testimonies, a writer becomes the witness to man.

CHAOTIC BEGINNINGS

Aleksandr Isayevich Solzhenitsyn was born on December 11, 1918—one year after the Russian czar was deposed in a violent revolution—in the small resort town of Kislovodsk in southern Russia. His father, Isaaki Solzhenitsyn, a former student at the University of Moscow who had served in the Russian army as an artillery officer, had been killed in a hunting accident six months earlier. His mother, Taissia Zakharovna Shcherbak, the daughter of a wealthy landowner of Ukrainian origin, was left to nurture her son alone in very difficult times. She eventually found a job as a typist-stenographer, and in 1924 she moved with her son to Rostov-on-Don, a large seaport in southern Russia.

The young Solzhenitsyn grew up in the years when the Communists were consolidating power in Russia and expanding that power by combining with neighboring nations to form the Union of Soviet Socialist Republics (USSR). The 1920s and 1930s saw the implementation of Soviet premier Joseph Stalin's collectivization policy, which confiscated lands from the rich and moderately wealthy peasants (*kulaks*) and placed agricultural production entirely in the hands of collective farms owned and supervised by the government. This policy led to shortages of food, starvation, and, consequently, massive deaths. Solzhenitsyn's family was not spared. The new regime expropriated the estate of his grandfather, Zakhar Shcherbak, a former peasant who had become a landowner. Deprived of its land, Solzhenitsyn's family suffered from poverty along with other formerly well-to-do Russians.

Young Aleksandr and his mother were forced to make do with what little they had. For example, one day in school he accidentally sat in some black ink, which left a large stain on his pants. Even after repeated washings, the ink spot would not disappear. He had to wear this pair of pants for several years before his mother could afford to buy him a new pair. The poverty and hardships of these years instilled in Aleksandr a habit of living simply, which stayed with him from then on.

BECOMING A WRITER

Despite the difficulty of his life, Aleksandr grew up loving literature. As a young child he read the works of such great Russian authors as Aleksandr Pushkin, Leo Tolstoy, Fyodor Dostoyevsky, Nikolay Gogol, and Ivan Turgenev, spending hours in the library of his Aunt Irina. Aleksandr's aunt was an important influence in his life. When he visited her on holidays and in the summer, she would tell him stories of the revolution, his forbears, and the Christian Orthodox Church, with its rich ceremonial life.

By age eight or nine, Aleksandr had visions of himself becoming one of three things: a general, priest, or writer. Certainly, he was intellectually gifted. As a young student, he was outstanding in both the sciences and the arts, and on one occasion he won a bicycle as an award for outstanding academic achievement.

As a high school student in the early 1930s, he was an ardent fan of Karl Marx and Vladimir Lenin, enlisting in the Young Pioneers, the organization of youngsters supervised by the Communist Party. During this period he also started writing poems, stories, and essays, and he kept a journal of his works. In 1936, not yet eighteen, he committed himself to a goal: writing about the Russian Revolution.

MARXISM, MARRIAGE, AND WAR

While young Solzhenitsyn wanted to pursue literature in college, Rostov-on-Don did not offer such a field, and his mother did not have the means to send him to Moscow. So, in 1936 he enrolled at Rostov University to study math and physics, subjects that also interested him. In the university, Solzhenitsyn continued to write and to study Marxism. He also actively participated in the activities of Komsomol, the organization of college students whose members were being eyed by the Communist Party establishment for advancement in the party's hierarchy. A child of the revolution, Solzhenitsyn was proud to be a part of the Communist establishment and wished to participate in achieving its goals.

It was at Rostov University that Solzhenitsyn met Natalya Reshetovskaya, a promising chemistry student and pianist. Even before graduating, he and Reshetovskaya married in 1940. Also while still at Rostov University, Solzhenitsyn studied by correspondence at the Institute of History, Philosophy, and Literature in Moscow, thus securing some literary education.

In October 1941 Nazi Germany attacked Russia. Solzhenitsyn enlisted in the army, was assigned to artillery school, and was sent to the Gorki region. In the field, he saw heavy combat, was promoted to captain, and was decorated twice. Solzhenitsyn was at the battlefront when his mother died of tuberculosis at the age of forty-seven in January 1944.

IMPRISONMENT AND EXILE

In February 1945 Solzhenitsyn's military career, which was beginning to shine, was cut short. He was arrested after intelligence authorities intercepted letters containing criticisms of Stalin that Solzhenitsyn had sent to a friend. A special board of the secret police sentenced Solzhenitsyn to eight years in prison. As was standard procedure during the Stalin era, Solzhenitsyn was not allowed to be present for his sentencing.

Solzhenitsyn served the initial phase of his sentence in several work camps around Moscow. In 1946, because of his skills as a mathematician, he was transferred to a *sharashka,* a research institute that doubles as a prison for intellectuals and scientists. He stayed there for four years in relatively good living conditions. This relatively easy life soon grew far more difficult, however.

In 1950, because of acts of noncooperation, he was moved from the research institute to a forced-labor camp in the town of Ekibastuz in Kazakhstan. There, he joined thousands of other victims of Stalin's regime—intellectuals, former military officers, laborers, students, and criminals. Solzhenitsyn worked alternately as a miner, bricklayer, and foundryman, and it was in the labor camp that he conceived *One Day in the Life of Ivan Denisovich*, basing the details of camp life on firsthand experience. In the camp he also began to be disillusioned with Marxism and began his conversion to Christianity. There, too, his conviction to write about the atrocities in the concentration camps arose, and he vowed to vindicate the lives of thousands of his countrymen who had died and suffered in the camps.

While in prison, he urged his wife to find another man so that she did not have to suffer being alone and could have an easier life. Although she wavered, she eventually formed a relationship in 1952 with Vsevolod Somov, a man who already had two children by a previous marriage.

In 1953 Solzhenitsyn's sentence was completed, but the authorities did not release him. Instead, he was ordered exiled to Kok-Terek, a village in southern Kazakhstan. There, he was allowed to work as a physics teacher in a local school. From March 1953 to June 1956, he served this exile.

In 1953 he became very ill and was found to have cancer. He was subsequently sent to Tashkent, the capital of the Uzbek region, where more modern equipment and more reliable medical services were available. The cancer was treated in 1954, and he eventually recovered. The experience would provide material for the novel *Cancer Ward*.

An Exile No More

In 1956, during the rule of Soviet premier Nikita Khrushchev, the Twentieth Congress of the Communist Party granted political amnesty to millions of prisoners and freed those living in exile. After eleven years in prisons, camps, and in exile, Solzhenitsyn was free to move where he pleased.

After his release from exile, Solzhenitsyn settled in Ryazan, a booming oil refinery city 115 miles southwest of Moscow. There, he found a job as a mathematics teacher. Reshetovskaya was about to marry Somov, but Solzhenitsyn asked his wife to remarry him, and they reunited.

After his imprisonment, Solzhenitsyn began to write, but he did not immediately go back to the epic of the Russian Revolution, the writing project he most wanted to embark on. He set this aside for what he saw as a more urgent task: exposing the gulag (concentration camp system), the millions who had died, the architects of the gulag, and Marxism itself.

Solzhenitsyn said later that he set out to resurrect his people's memory, believing it was his duty as a writer to tell the truth. He began to write *One Day in the Life of Ivan Denisovich.*

A HIGH POINT

The truth started to come out in 1962 with the publication of Solzhenitsyn's novel in the Soviet literary journal *Novy Mir.* The novel got past the censors through the help of Aleksandr Tvardovsky, a noted poet and the editor in chief of *Novy Mir,* who personally brought it to the attention of Premier Nikita Khrushchev. In a single day, ninety-five thousand issues of the magazine were snapped up by eager Russians, and Solzhenitsyn, an unknown writer until that time, gained instant fame.

While Khrushchev favored de-Stalinization, the Soviet leader often vacillated between liberalization and repression. He condemned Stalin's terrorist methods and excesses, but he was also determined to preserve the power structure Stalin had built. On the other hand, Khrushchev's efforts were often opposed and resented by conservatives. In this atmosphere, conservative party leaders soon attacked Solzhenitsyn's work. Although Tvardovsky and other noted writers defended him, the fall of Khrushchev from power in 1964, which signaled the resurfacing of Soviet conservatism and censorship, dealt a blow to Solzhenitsyn's career.

In spite of growing pressure from his critics, in 1964 Solzhenitsyn began work on *The Gulag Archipelago,* a scathing documentation of the atrocities in the concentration camps. To avoid trouble from the Soviet authorities, he kept it a secret. A large work, he knew it would take him years to finish. His plan was to have it published only in 1975, by which time he thought censorship in the Soviet Union would have eased.

The harassment and attacks from the authorities became more frequent, but Solzhenitsyn had a circle of influential supporters and friends who pushed for the publication of his work. By 1965 he had completed two more novels, *The First Circle* and *Cancer Ward,* in which he continued his self-assigned task of exposing the truth about Soviet society. *The First Circle,* which alludes to Dante's *Inferno,* portrays the intricate and systematic entrapment of individuals practiced by Stalin's regime and the triumph of will and spirit of the novel's characters over that repression. *Cancer Ward,* often read as a metaphor for the totalitarian state, further extends the idea of individual freedom. The main character, Oleg Kostoglotov—a former camp inmate turned cancer patient who has been consigned to permanent exile—actually finds liberation through acts of goodness and his encounter with death.

In spite of the influence of Solzhenitsyn's friends, the two novels were denied publication in *Novy Mir*. However, in 1968 copies eventually were published through the unofficial process called *samizdat*, which translates literally as "self-publishing" but also means the illegal distribution of censored material. As a result, the political and literary establishments in the Soviet Union launched a campaign to discredit Solzhenitsyn. Attacks against his works and his person surfaced in the pages of *Pravda*, the Communist Party's official newspaper. His manuscripts and archives were later seized by the KGB, the secret police.

AT WAR WITH THE ESTABLISHMENT

Solzhenitsyn refused to be silenced, and in response to the attacks, he wrote an open letter to the Fourth Writers' Congress, an important meeting of the Writers' Union, the official literary organization of which he was a member. In his letter, he appealed for the abolition of censorship and the protection of writers. By addressing his letter to this official body, Solzhenitsyn was protesting a specific policy of the literary establishment, but in the view of Soviet authorities, he might as well be criticizing the government directly.

Meanwhile, more of Solzhenitsyn's manuscripts began to reach the outside world. In 1968 *The First Circle* was published in German, and *Cancer Ward* was published in Italy and England. The tug-of-war between Solzhenitsyn and the Soviet establishment was reaching new heights, and many observers believed that a case was being built by the government to finally arrest him.

The year 1968 marked a change in Solzhenitsyn's personal life when he met Natalya Svetlova, a young mathematician who became part of his clandestine network of assistants and supporters and later his lover. The relationship, which was kept secret at first, eventually came to the attention of Reshetovskaya, who said later that about this time he seemed to change—that he began having affairs with younger women.

As attacks from the establishment escalated, Solzhenitsyn

actually started fearing for his life. He knew he could suffer the fate of other dissidents before him: arrest, confinement in a psychiatric ward, torture, and eventual disappearance. He began to move from one place to another, relying more and more on a group of supporters, mostly women, who typed his manuscripts, distributed them in samizdat, organized his files, maintained his archives, and hid his works.

In 1969 Solzhenitsyn was finally expelled from the Writers' Union. The expulsion made him a renegade in the eyes of the establishment. He was thus transformed into a pariah, and his access to social security, pension, health and medical benefits, as well as libraries (all of which he enjoyed as a union member) was canceled. Detractors accused him of being a tool of the imperialists, a slanderer of the Soviet Union, and a liar. In an issue of *Pravda* in December 1970, *Cancer Ward* and *The First Circle* were described as "lampoons of the Soviet Union which blacken the achievements of our fatherland and the dignity of the Soviet people."

THE NOBEL PRIZE

The official condemnation of Solzhenitsyn at home only served to enhance his image abroad. Letters of support, coming from important political and literary figures in Europe and the United States, condemned his expulsion from the Writers' Union and appealed for his reinstatement. Then, in 1970, he was awarded the Nobel Prize for literature, the most prestigious award a writer can receive. Solzhenitsyn, however, chose not to attend the award ceremonies in Stockholm, as he feared that he would not be allowed to reenter the Soviet Union. The Soviet regime reacted to the news by denouncing the Swedish Academy, which awards the prize, and by calling Solzhenitsyn a "run-of-the-mill" writer. So harsh was the Soviet government's response that supporters and friends feared that Solzhenitsyn's arrest was now just a matter of time. Also at this time, Solzhenitsyn's personal life was in turmoil: His divorce from Reshetovskaya was pending, and Svetlova was expecting a baby.

Throughout these tumultuous years, Solzhenitsyn had continued working on the first part of his planned opus on the Russian Revolution, *August 1914.* This was just the first in a series of volumes in a saga he titled *The Red Wheel.* In 1971, when this first volume was completed and was subsequently denied local publication by the authorities, Solzhenitsyn authorized its publication in the West. The main character, Colonel Vorotyntsev, is isolated by Soviet authorities after attempting to tell the truth about the government's disastrous mismanagement of the Russian efforts in World War I. As he had in other novels, Solzhenitsyn portrayed his character as being spiritually liberated through his heroic act, even though it cost him his privileged position.

In March 1972, as he began to see that the smear campaign being waged against him by the Soviet authorities would not stop, Solzhenitsyn granted his first interview to Western reporters. In this interview, he denied the stories that were being disseminated: that during the war he had surrendered to the Germans and that he had been a collaborator with the Nazis. He also said that people close to him, including his wife, were being dismissed from their jobs in an effort to harass and punish him.

CONFISCATION OF *THE GULAG ARCHIPELAGO*

Meanwhile, the KGB had learned about the existence of a copy of the manuscript of *The Gulag Archipelago*, which was in the hands of a former assistant, Elizaveta Voronyanskaya. After five days of interrogation, she revealed where the manuscript was hidden. The KGB offered Solzhenitsyn a deal. In exchange for the publication of *Cancer Ward* in the Soviet Union, he would have to delay the release of *The Gulag Archipelago* for twenty years. Although he had by this time divorced Natalya Reshetovskaya, the KGB used her in these negotiations. Solzhenitsyn was outraged and accused his former wife of collaborating with the KGB.

With the disclosure of the existence of *The Gulag Archipelago*, Solzhenitsyn decided he could no longer afford to hold to his plan of publishing the book in 1975. He authorized the publication in Paris of the first two parts of the novel in December 1973 and the whole book in the United States in 1974. A vicious campaign of vilification from Soviet authorities followed.

In the face of insults, continued harassment, and threats from USSR's political establishment, Solzhenitsyn remained determined. At times, however, he succumbed to despair and even entertained thoughts of suicide, especially after the confiscation of his manuscripts. Still, he always managed to resist the pressures, both external and internal. Later, he noted, "My point of departure (was) that I did not belong to myself alone, that my literary destiny was not just my own, but that of millions who had not lived to scrawl or gasp or croak the truth about their lot as jailbirds."

AN EXILE ONCE MORE

Matters came to a head when Solzhenitsyn was arrested on February 12, 1974, and was charged with treason. Solzhenitsyn, however, was too widely renowned for the authorities to simply imprison him. The Soviet Supreme Court issued a decree stripping him of his citizenship and deported him to West Germany. Eventually, he made his way to Switzerland, where he was joined by his family—Svetlova, the three children they had by this time, and a daughter from Svetlova's first marriage. For the next two years, the family lived in Zurich.

In Switzerland, Solzhenitsyn feared that the KGB would continue to harass him and his family and that he would not have the privacy he needed, so in 1976 he decided to move to the United States. Bringing his family with him, he settled on a fifty-acre estate in rural Cavendish, Vermont. The estate's high walls and security monitors ensured his privacy and his family's safety. He said that he had chosen the place because of its rural character and the long winters, which reminded him of Russia.

Part of the huge compound was a building that housed his archives and the All-Russian Memoir Library. The latter was part of a project that aimed to rescue the collective memory of the Russian people by collecting materials from Russia's past, particularly memoirs. Solzhenitsyn believed that the government during the Soviet era had drawn a false picture of Russia, and he vowed it was his duty to help correct it. He appealed to people to send him their materials, which he promised would be organized and made available to scholars. Solzhenitsyn's goal was to eventually move the library to a major city in central Russia.

TIRADE AGAINST THE WEST

To the consternation of some in the West, Solzhenitsyn proved to be a critic of more than just the Soviet system. In lectures he was invited to give, he often criticized the United States and the rest of the West as being morally weak and suffering from "spiritual impotence." During the commencement at Harvard University in 1978, he noted the West's failings and moral decline, the failure of détente (the U.S. policy of warming relations with the USSR) to bring about significant change in the Soviet Union, and the inappropriateness of democracy for governing Russia. He concluded his message by recommending a solution to the West's malady: a return to morality and Christian values. The speech, which was broadcast live on television, was applauded by the audience but drew much criticism from intellectuals and liberal thinkers.

The life Solzhenitsyn settled into in Vermont was a spartan one in which he isolated himself from American society, whose preoccupation with material goods he reviled. He concentrated on writing, which he pursued with dogged determination and intense focus.

Meanwhile, change was underway in Solzhenitsyn's homeland. In the late eighties, Soviet president Mikhael Gorbachev launched radical reforms in the USSR, primarily his twin policies of glasnost (openness) and perestroika (restructuring). These reforms led to the lifting of censorship in the Soviet Union. Accordingly, publication of Solzhenitsyn's works, notably *The Gulag Archipelago*, resumed. Other developments affected Solzhenitsyn directly. In 1989 he was reinstated in the Writers' Union. Then, in 1990, his citizenship was restored, and in 1991 the treason charges against him were dropped.

FREE AT LAST

In 1994 his deliverance finally came: At age seventy-five, he returned to Russia along with his family. Upon his arrival, he was received by no less than Russian president Boris Yeltsin. Once again a hero in his homeland, he was invited to address the Duma, the lower house of the Russian Parliament.

Solzhenitsyn continued, however, to be a gadfly. In June 1998 *Russia in Ruin*, which criticizes aspects of Russian life after the fall of Communism, came out. Initially, only five thousand copies of the book were ordered, but after these were sold, another five thousand copies were made available.

Solzhenitsyn refuses to be silent. From his home near Moscow, he occasionally lashes out at the materialism of his countrymen, the failings of Russia's fledgling democracy, and the corruption infecting his country's leaders. In a speech, he said, "We are doing everything to destroy Russia. We have no market, no democracy, a wild predatory capitalism is being built here."

In 1998, at age eighty, Solzhenitsyn published *November 1916*, the second volume of *The Red Wheel*, the trilogy that started with *August 1914*. Disrupted by decades of exile, the life work that he had set for himself when he was only eighteen years old is now at last coming to fruition.

Today, Solzhenitsyn stands as one of the most-read writers of the twentieth century. One biographer points out that the first volume of *The Gulag Archipelago* sold between 8 and 10 million copies in the early eighties. This same biographer notes that, as of 1972, Solzhenitsyn was tied with Shakespeare for the number of languages into which his works had been translated.

Speaking of the legacy of Solzhenitsyn, Alya N. Altynina, the book review editor of the prestigious *Literaturnaya Gazeta* in Moscow, says, "He has gone down in history and will no doubt be studied as a classical writer of the Soviet times."

A former prime minister, Yegor Gaidar, sums up Solzhenitsyn's place in Russia: "The influence of Solzhenitsyn on Russian literature and in Russian history was enormous—incomparable to any other writer in this century." For other Russians, Solzhenitsyn's impact is more personal. To Zoya Marchenko, age ninety-one, who spent more than twenty years in labor camps, Solzhenitsyn is a "symbol of bravery, honesty, and truth," and he sees Solzhenitsyn's continued writing as "fulfilling his duty to the dead."

Today, Solzhenitsyn's compatriots do not read his works in large numbers. Many find his ideas conservative and find it difficult to identify with his ultranationalist views and with his anti-Communism. Younger Russians and other readers may not recognize the colossal magnitude of his work, but his legacy is solid. Writing about freedom, Solzhenitsyn has weathered all kinds of repression, but he, his heroes, and his books have prevailed.

CHARACTERS AND PLOT

THE CHARACTERS

Ivan Denisovich Shukhov. Prisoner Number S854, Shukhov has spent eight years in the camp. During World War II, he was captured by the Germans but was able to escape. The Soviets suspected him of spying for the Germans, charged him with treason, and sent him to Ust-Izhma.

Alyoshka the Baptist (also Alyosha, Aleshka). One of the most dependable members of Shukhov's squad, he survives through his religious faith. He finds time to pray and hides his Bible in a brick wall.

Tyurin (also Tiurin). The leader of the 104th squad, Tyurin is respected because of his strength and fairness. He was a former officer discharged and imprisoned after authorities found that his father was a rich peasant.

Caesar (also Tzesar, Tsezar). A former cameraman and intellectual, Caesar bribes the right people to enjoy some privileges (e.g., a warm room and office work); he receives two parcels from home every month.

Buynovsky the Captain (also Buinovsky, Buinovskii). He is a former naval officer and is new in the camp and thus doesn't know his way around. Used to giving orders, he finds it difficult to adjust to the harsh camp life.

Fetyukov (also Fetiukov). A member of Shukhov's squad, Fetyukov has almost no pride left; he spends a lot of time scavenging, his way of survival.

Vdovushkin. He is the young medical assistant who mans the dispensary. He has studied literature and aspires to become a writer.

Lieutenant Volcovoy (also Volkovoi). A disciplinary officer who looks at prisoners "like a wolf," he used to carry a whip and requires prisoners to strip for body searches.

Pavlo. He is the assistant to Tyurin and comes from western Ukraine. He cares about the survival of the squad and helps weaker members while they are adjusting to camp life.

Senka Klevshin. A member of the squad, Klevshin is deaf and has spent a difficult time in a German camp. The squad somehow accommodates his weakness.

The Tartar. A guard at the camp who does everything by the book; he looks for people to pick on.

Two Estonians. Two men, one a fisherman and the other a former college student, who are very close to each other. Like brothers, they rely on each other for survival.

Gopchik. A young Ukrainian, Gopchik adapts easily to the camp rules.

Kilgas. He is a mason who has been in the camp for two years and likes to make jokes. He receives two parcels from home every month.

Kusyomin (also Kuziomin). As Shukhov's first squad leader at Ust-Izhma, Kusyomin teaches Shukhov about survival. He hates squealers.

"One and a Half" Ivan. He is a guard at Shukhov's current camp. He looks tough, but Shukhov considers him one of the "safer" guards.

The Latvian. He is a prisoner who sells tobacco, one of the last pleasures allowed in the camp.

Der. He is a foreman who is rumored to have worked in a ministry in Moscow and is always looking over the shoulder of prisoners. He wants to become an engineer.

The Moldavian. A prisoner who was missing in the lineup during a roll call, he was found asleep in the worksite.

The Limper. A mess orderly who is disabled, he uses a club to hit anyone who comes up the steps without his permission.

Mess Chief. He is one of the prisoners who doesn't wear a tag.

THE PLOT

It is a day in January 1951 in a prison camp. The temperature is below freezing. Ivan Denisovich Shukhov, prisoner number S854, does not rise after the 5:00 A.M. reveille: He isn't feeling well. He lingers in his bunk—even though he knows he could be locked up in a punishment cell for three days—hoping he will be sent to the hospital. Shukhov, who has served eight years out of a ten-year sentence, is lucky: The warder only makes him scrub the guardroom floor. From here he goes to the mess hall, where he eats his breakfast bowl of stew, which Fetyukov, the prisoner with the lowest status in the squad, has saved for him.

Before the roll call, Shukhov goes to the dispensary to ask if he can be excused from work. Vdovushkin, the young medic aspiring to become a poet, takes his temperature, which is too low to allow Shukhov to be excused; he sends Shukhov back to work.

Back in the barracks, Pavlo, a western Ukrainian who is a member of Shukhov's work squad, gives Shukhov his bread ration. Shukhov stuffs half of it into a hole in his mattress and the other half into a pocket that he has sewn into his jacket. The squad leader, Tyurin, a former military officer who is an old hand in the camp, orders them to file out for roll call. Shukhov admires the boss's way of managing the squad.

SHUKHOV'S FIRST TRIUMPH FOR THE DAY

After roll call, Shukhov notices the faded prisoner number on his uniform. He asks one of the camp artists to repaint it. He then returns to his squad and finds Caesar, a rich prisoner who receives two packages a month from home, smoking a cigarette. Fetyukov eagerly waits for the cigarette butt, but Caesar gives it to Shukhov. Shukhov considers beating Fetyukov to the cigarette butt his first triumph that day.

Before the members of the work gang go out to the construction site, the guards frisk them. Lieutenant Volkovoy, the disciplinary officer, looks on. The workers are then turned over to the guards, who are equipped with guns and dogs. They march out toward the construction site, where icy wind and a stretch of seemingly endless snow greet them. The gang's worksite is a repair shop. Tyurin tells his group he was able to bribe the camp leaders with a pound of salt, so the squad doesn't have to be sent to another worksite, the Socialist Community Development, where workers toil in the open in the brutal cold.

The squad's assignment is to lay bricks on the second-story walls of an unfinished power plant. But first, Shukhov and Kilgas have to find some materials to cover the windows in the generator room to keep the place warm. Here, the men will mix mortar. The two go out, and when they return, they carry roofing material stolen from another site. Shukhov is also asked to fix the stove. The gang spends the whole morning preparing for the bricklaying.

At lunch break, the men go to the mess hall, where

Shukhov and his gang enjoy their meal of mush. The squad gets two extra bowls for its work, one of which the squad gives to Shukhov. He counts this another victory. The other bowl is given to Captain Buynovsky, a former military officer and a new prisoner who has yet to learn the "ropes."

After lunch, Shukhov finds Caesar and a camp supervisor discussing director Sergey Eisenstein's film *Ivan the Terrible.* Shukhov hands a bowl of mush to Caesar, but the film enthusiast does not even look at him. Shukhov returns to the worksite, and on the way he finds a chunk of metal sticking out of the snow; he thinks he can make use of it some other time.

When he returns to his work gang, he borrows a cigarette from another prisoner, an Estonian. After smoking the cigarette, he gives the butt to Alyoshka, the Baptist, instead of to Fetyukov, whom he dislikes.

FINDING BROTHERHOOD IN LABOR

The mood of the squad brightens as they start to work. They know that if they do their job well, they can earn extra bread rations. In the afternoon, Shukhov and Kilgas begin to lay bricks, and after some time, Shukhov and the men, including Pavlo, Captain Buynovsky, Fetyukov, and Senka, concentrate on the work, set a fast pace, and even find a sort of brotherhood in their labors. Even after the whistle signaling the end of the workday sounds, the men continue to work. Shukhov even lingers at the walls before they line up for the march back to the camp. It is now dark and the moon is rising.

During the count, the guards find one prisoner is missing. Two men go back to the worksite to find him. He is found on the scaffolding in a building where he had gotten warm and fallen asleep. The prisoners shout insults at him; they've lost a half hour and may be the last group back to the camp. Squad 104 marches fast, though, and beats the other groups. At the gates, the prisoners drop the bundles of scrap firewood they had collected at the construction site before they are once again frisked by the guards. Shukhov succeeds in hiding in one of his mittens the piece of steel he had picked up earlier.

Once inside the compound, Shukhov decides not to go straight to the mess hall. He rushes to the package room and stands in line on behalf of Caesar. He sees this as an opportunity for a future reward. Later, when Caesar makes it to the line, Shukhov asks him if he wants his dinner brought to his office. Caesar tells Shukhov he may have it.

Before he goes to the mess hall, Shukhov runs quickly to the barracks to visit his bunk; he wants to be sure the chunk of bread he hid in the morning is safe. Then he goes to the mess hall and, through skillful maneuvering, gets his gang's supper bowls, careful to assign for himself the two bowls with the most food in them. Shukhov is pleased that tonight he will have a large supper—his bowl and the one from Caesar. The squad gets its extra bread; Shukhov selects a crusty piece.

After supper he goes to another part of the compound to buy tobacco from Kilgas, the Latvian, using money he received from doing odd jobs. When he goes back to the barracks, he sees that Caesar has opened his package. Shukhov offers Caesar his ration of bread, part of the supper he missed; Caesar tells him to keep it. Once again, Shukhov counts this as a small victory. He climbs into his bunk and relishes his bread. Shukhov then pays back the tobacco he had borrowed earlier from the Estonian in the worksite at noon.

Caesar shares his food from his parcel, which includes cheese and sausages, with Captain Buynovsky. Shukhov pretends he does not see the food. When they are about to eat the sausage, Caesar asks to borrow Shukhov's knife, and he lends it to them.

HAPPY AT THE END OF THE DAY

The squad is called out for the evening roll call while Caesar is eating his food in the open. Shukhov is concerned that someone might steal it while they go for the count. Shukhov offers to guard Caesar's parcel by rushing back quickly to the barracks after the count. When they return, Shukhov places his boots near the stove and guards both Caesar's package and his boots.

Caesar thanks Shukhov, who returns to his bunk to prepare his bed for sleep. Just as most of the prisoners have gotten warm, the squad is called out for a second roll call. As they move out, Caesar hands Shukhov some food, including biscuits and a sausage, thanking him. Shukhov offers to hide the rest of his parcel in his mattress.

After the check, the prisoners are back in their bunks. Shukhov discusses religion with Alyoshka, the Baptist. Shukhov admires Alyoshka's faith and meekness, but he thinks the Baptist does not know how to survive. He hands him a biscuit; Alyoshka thanks him.

Shukhov begins to chew the piece of sausage, savoring its juices, and counts all of the good things that have happened to him during the day. Shukhov falls asleep, almost happy because he has succeeded not only in surviving but in gaining small victories as well.

CHAPTER 1

Themes in *One Day*

A Quest for Truth, Justice, and Charity

Hélène Zamoyska

In *One Day,* Aleksandr Solzhenitsyn sets out to tell the truth about the Soviet concentration camps. In his quest, he contributes to the "grand tradition" of Russian literature, which according to author Hélène Zamoyska, is concerned with truth, justice, and solidarity. What sets Solzhenitsyn apart from the best Russian writers, Zamoyska asserts, is that his narrative is pared down to essentials, without embellishments such as loud protest and elaborate opinion. Zamoyska, a professor of Slavic literatures at the University of Toulouse at the time of writing, has written extensively on Russian literature.

[Aleksandr Solzhenitsyn adheres to the so-called Grand Tradition in Russian literature], a certain inner attitude towards life and mankind which has always and in every period characterized the best Russian artists dedicated to the discovery of truth. . . .

Solzhenitsyn is the witness of an era "not lacking in tears" (to use his own phrase), and it is precisely the most tragic aspects which he describes: the concentration camps. . . .

Solzhenitsyn has joined a current which seeks to reestablish the truth where it has been silent or distorted for so long; but he is better able than other writers to observe and describe what he sees. In this he remains faithful to the best traditions of what the Soviets call "critical realism."

Nothing escapes his penetrating vision. The conditions in which not only the inmates of labor camps live—but also the free wartime population and the peasants in the center of Russia ten years ago—are depicted with pitiless exactitude but without an overabundance of details. Their day-to-day existence unfolds, dominated by a ceaseless struggle against three enemies: cold, hunger, and exhaustion.

From "Solzhenitsyn and the Grand Tradition," by Hélène Zamoyska, translated by David Halperin from "Soljenitsyne et la Grande Tradition," *La Table Ronde*, vol. 185 (1963), in *Critical Essays and Documentary Materials*, edited by John B. Dunlop, Richard Haugh, and Alexis Klimoff (Belmont, MA: Nordland, 1973). Reprinted by permission of David Halperin.

Hunger, the obsession of prisoners condemned to a maximum amount of work on a minimum of food ("But come to think of it, they ate four days for every five they worked") is a constant and unrelieved torment.

> The prisoners were at their coldest and hungriest when they checked in through these gates in the evening, and their bowl of hot and watery soup without any fat was like rain in a drought. They gulped it down. They cared more for this bowlful than freedom, or for their life in years gone by and years to come. . . .

There is exhaustion, so persistent that one falls asleep at the slightest breath of warmth and fails to make roll call, like the "real" Moldavian spy who gets himself beaten to a pulp by the guards and his fellow inmates for making them wait for him in the cold. In order to protect oneself from fatigue, one has to make the most economical use of one's strength. Thus Shukhov notes the transformation taking place in the newly-arrived Buinovskii "from a bossy, loudmouth naval officer into a slow-moving and cagey prisoner. He'd have to be like this if he wanted to get through his twenty-five years in camp."

SYSTEMATIC CRUELTY

These are forces which are at all times hostile to man—whether they are systematically exploited in camp to dehumanize him, triumph spontaneously in the cataclysm of war, or result from criminal neglect on the part of the authorities. Whatever the reason for which they are unleashed, they have to be put down. Only those who know the ropes manage to achieve this, either through theft or by using their wits. . . . It is a question of life or death and even the most honest (Shukhov in the camp) have frequent recourse to such methods without scruple.

But such agonizing living conditions stem to a large extent from certain kinds of social or human relationships. And so the society described by Solzhenitsyn, or rather the segments of it he portrays, are regulated by cruel laws: the struggle for survival and the tyranny of the strong. . . .

Nevertheless, the picture which Solzhenitsyn draws of societal relationships cannot be reduced to some formula—and a rather simplistic one at that—according to which superiors automatically become tyrants. For the peasant Shukhov, it is true, official authority is a sort of power that is foreign to his world, as his naive reaction (when Buinovskii informs him that the Soviet government has altered the day-time by decree) illustrates: "Did the sun come under their laws too?" But he is by no means an anarchist. He agrees without reservation to work under the command of capable and dedicated individuals. This is the case with his foreman Tiurin who protects his subordinates, arranges to obtain supplementary rations for them, and puts his shoulder to the wheel. "The higher-ups had a job to get a prisoner to work even in working hours, but your boss only had to say the word, even if it was the meal break, and you worked."

But above all it should be stressed that Solzhenitsyn's point of view is not that of a sociologist or of a politician. It is the attitude of a writer who is interested in the psychological source of human acts and of social systems. In this light, the forces of oppression appear complex and subtle, because they are rooted in man's nature and in the ideas which guide him. . . .

Solzhenitsyn does not tell the reader all this in so many words; in fact he hardly comments at all. . . . It is up to the reader to interpret and to judge—the author does not condemn. Except perhaps for the bureaucrats and selfish profiteers, is anyone really guilty? The faults, the errors, the cruelties attain such phantasmagoric proportions that they exceed human understanding and seem to be the work of some mysterious evil force that makes a fool of man. For all is paradox and pure nonsense: Shukhov did not allow himself to be captured by the Germans and rejoined Soviet lines. That was sufficient to condemn him to forced labor as a spy. His only fault was to have been too patriotic . . . Buinovskii is another sort of "spy." He received a gift from a British admiral with whom he had served as a liaison officer during the war. The price of that gift: twenty-five years of hard labor! . . .

The miracle is that man can keep from sinking to the level of animals, even under the appalling conditions to which he is subjected. Solzhenitsyn bears witness to this miracle; in fact, one could safely assert that it is the true theme of his stories. Not that he idealizes these prisoners, so much like the ones he himself has rubbed shoulders with. . . . He knows their weaknesses, but he appreciates their greatness.

How strong is man's basic sense of personal dignity, in spite of all his humiliations! This is apparent in his most humble gestures—his manner of eating, for example; despite the cold, Shukhov cannot bring himself to eat the scraps of food put before him without first removing his cap. And Iu-81, that tall, toothless old man, who has never been freed, doubtless a former noble whose "worn-out face was dark and looked like it had been hewed out of stone" is the only one to sit up straight, without hunching over his rations! Or again, the Ukrainians from the Carpathians who, before eating, make the sign of the Cross, whereas "the Russians didn't even remember which hand you cross yourself with," as Shukhov remarks.

This self-respect rules out certain kinds of behavior. In spite of the longing that grips him, Shukhov will never stoop to pick up a cigarette-butt, even though there are moments when he would rather have a cigarette "than his freedom." Never will he beg for a part of his more fortunate neighbors' food packages. And never in all his forty years has he learned to grease anyone's palm, no matter whose, even in camp.

One could hardly ask for more spectacular gestures from a prisoner: Buinovskii, a naval captain recently arrived in the camp, reacts with virulence against an order which seems to him outrageous: "You've no right to strip people in the cold!" he tells the guards during the frisking, "You don't know Article Nine of the Criminal Code! . . . You're not Soviet people," the Captain barks, "You're not Communists!" But he is a novice—such protests earn him ten days in the cooler, without heat or warm food, except once every three days. He will learn to his sorrow that in camp it is best to keep quiet.

The creative instinct, deeply rooted in man, persists with astonishing vitality. It is expressed by man's manner of working. Solzhenitsyn is free from a false pathos which would glorify labor as such and make it the meaning and purpose of existence. The simple men of his stories are not taken in by the glitter of fine phrases; the way these phrases have been used has served only to tarnish them. Did not the inmates of German concentration camps also hear the slogan *Arbeit macht frei* repeated? Shukhov doesn't fall for it: he does not at all appreciate the methods of "work therapy" practised by the camp doctor. ("What he didn't understand was that work has killed many a horse.") . . . He knows all too well that work can be an instrument of enslavement which degrades man and virtually transforms him into a beast of burden: "There's work and work. It's like the two ends of a stick. If you're working for human beings, then do a real job of it, but if you work for dopes, then you just go through the motions."

But he knows the good end of the "stick" perfectly well. Once he is led by a foreman he respects, Shukhov puts all his energy into carrying out his job well. And the whole work gang acts the same way, each man revealing his character and his worth in their common labors, since work for Shukhov is an infallible test: Buinovskii, worn out as he is, goes at his work with courage: "To the Captain, camp work was like the navy. ('If you're told to do something, then get down to it!')" Fetiukov, the "slacker," always tries to "get out of it." Aleshka the Baptist is an ideal co-worker—a "lamb." Shukhov himself cannot stand to rush anything. He is so absorbed by his work on the wall that he loses track of time and nearly comes late to the roll call. "Shukhov was kind of funny about these things . . . He still worried about every little thing and about all kinds of work." A significant detail: Ivan Denisovich is the sort of man who, though he does not permit himself to steal anything for his own benefit, filches a trowel which he keeps carefully hidden, so that he will be able to do "a really fine job." You have to read those marvellous pages in which the author portrays Shukhov as possessed by the giddy joy of building. . . .

SOLIDARITY AMONG THE PRISONERS

Finally, one striking trait emerges from all these stories. Although the hardships of life encourage egotism in some, they also stimulate altruism in others. Often, it is true, the one and the other coexist or alternate. . . .

Such mutual aid is powerfully evident in the camp. Those who have experienced total deprivation know the price of an additional hundred grams of bread, or a cigarette. Windfalls of this sort are a great occasion. Although Shukhov covets it for himself, he nonetheless approves of Pavlo's giving an extra serving to Buinovskii, who cannot believe his eyes. Should not one help him get accustomed to the place?

Such solidarity is also the bond which unites the work gang and makes it into a new family. Thus, Sen'ka waits for Shukhov, who was delayed at the power plant, and runs the risk of being seriously punished for the delay together with him, but "he wasn't the kind to leave you in the lurch." In the same brigade, Aleshka is always ready to do a favor, with an absolute selflessness that impresses Shukhov: "If only everybody in the world was like that, Shukhov would be that way too. If some one asked you, why not help him out? They were right on that, these people.". . .

These manifestations of pure altruism are difficult to discern, rare, and become exceptional when they are practised with the lack of self-interest of an Aleshka. But the very fact of their existence is sufficient to remind men that the law of the jungle where "big fish eat little ones" is opposed by another law which lifts man above bestiality: "Thou shalt love thy neighbor as thyself."

THE GRAND TRADITION

The Grand Tradition is first and foremost that of respect for Truth. It is in performing this demanding task that the greatest Russian writers have wielded their talent, and it is this very factor that makes them alive and close to us today. Like them, Solzhenitsyn does not invent life according to theoretical formulae; he describes it as he has known and felt it—violent, full of absurd and bloody misunderstandings, oppressive. His personal experience confers a poignant authenticity on his prose, and yet, it is not only personal impressions that he endeavors to convey to his readers; he also wants to share with us what he has discovered during his terrible years: namely, human beings who are worthy of the name. Thus, he disguises himself behind his characters in order to avoid serving as a screen between us and them. And we see them parade before our eyes, struggle, suffer, resist—each one different. Some are scoundrels, others drown in egoism, many help each other, some even achieve saintliness. The author condemns no one, except the "rapacious."

He manages to sustain this truthfulness in his portrayal of life and men by a form of narration purified of all superfluous commentary, of all emphasis. Solzhenitsyn writes only of what is essential, and the entire framework of life is carefully structured to bring out the character and the reactions of men. Their physical aspect is barely sketched in. On the other hand we see their gestures, perceive their attitudes, hear the crude and broken speech of the prisoners, the colorful language of the peasants. We distinguish the tone of their voices, their smiles, we witness their thoughts. In short, we know everything that reveals the quality of their souls.

And then the narration continues—simple, laconic, almost dry because of its starkness, interrupted here and there by an image shot through with emotion. . . .

JUSTICE FOR ALL

The picture Solzhenitsyn paints is black, and many readers will turn away from it, protesting that it does not give a complete description of Soviet life. Solzhenitsyn, however, does not make any such claim. [However,] he is not afraid to shake up the self-satisfied consciences of hypocrites and indecent optimists, whether the cause of their attitude be indifference or voluntary blindness. He remembers that a Russian writer in the service of Truth also serves Justice. Are not these two ideas closely linked in the Russian language, where the word *pravda* [truth] signified justice in former times? And to do justice to "the humiliated and the wronged" of our era, to those who, for so long now, have been systematically ignored or crushed in silence, is precisely to rejoin the grand, interrupted tradition of [Leo] Tolstoy and Dostoevsky. . . .

Although Solzhenitsyn's pity is primarily directed towards victims, he is humane to all, without any illusions concerning humanity, but also without hatred. Every man, whoever he may be, is, he feels, worthy of respect. It is this open-heartedness that earned Turgenev, Tolstoy, Chekhov, Gorkii, and many others their universal reputation. Solzhenitsyn does not parcel out his understanding according to any particular hierarchy: all are equal in misery. . . .

One's social origins are no guarantee of good or bad conduct: one finds a certain nobility of soul in Shukhov the peasant [as well as] Buinovskii the officer. . . .

Neither is there any chauvinism in this man who is Russian in every fiber of his being: Shukhov speaks with admiration of the Latvians, Estonians, and Ukrainians with whom he is thrown together. One could even say that all the non-Russians he portrays are models of dignity and courage. . . .

True respect for others and for their convictions—here is a quality most rare in contemporary Soviet literature. Apart from Pasternak, it is difficult to mention any writer who, in alluding to believers, does not make them into caricatures or objects of our compassion. . . .

This return to a sense of the human, with all that it entails of respect for others, of tolerance in heart and mind for what is different from us (a tolerance which obviously has nothing to do with "non-resistance to evil") constitutes not a disavowal of that which is near and dear, but suggests rather a rootedness in one's own country. Solzhenitsyn gives proof of this. . . .

Solzhenitsyn does not idealize his people, yet, deep within him, his country's secular traditions of true goodness and charity are maintained. Such ancient currents have a renewed freshness today, in this world . . . torn by hateful fanaticism, mutilated by sectarianism, . . . and invaded more and more by . . . materialism. . . . These currents constitute, in fact, the very fountainhead of life. Shukhov and his comrades . . . have all come to tell us that these qualities still well up within the Russian people, but they are concealed, and in order to discern them amid the struggles, bitterness, and agonizing injustices of [the] age, one must refine that "inner eye."

Moral Choices and Small Victories

Steven Allaback

Author Steven Allaback calls Shukhov "a hero only by
a hair," careful not to stoop as he waits, for example,
for a cigarette butt from a fellow prisoner. Shukhov
finds luxury in a pair of leather boots that comes his
way, but when he loses them again he does not succumb to despair. In his quest for small victories, he
makes sure he neither grovels nor offends his fellow
inmates. Allaback was a professor of English at the
University of California in Santa Barbara at the time of
writing. He has written articles and stories for *Prairee
Schooner, Ascent, Four Quarters, Ohio Review,* and
other journals.

I would like to begin this commentary by dismissing an approach to *One Day in the Life of Ivan Denisovich* which students of modernism, politics, catastrophe, and irony may be
tempted to follow. It might be put something like this:

Although the novel begins with Ivan Denisovich Shukhov
ill and ends with him "almost happy," his illness having
vanished during what appears to be a very good day, his
morning illness is actually psychological and symbolic of his
condition as a prisoner-citizen in an unspeakably ghastly
Soviet institution. His restoration to health and happiness by
evening is merely a rhetorical device and the greatest irony
in a novel full of ironies. Because he is lucky enough to lose
himself in a job of satisfying work for a change, because he
accidentally discovers a potentially valuable chunk of steel
in the snow, because he happens to receive far more to eat
this day than his usual pitiful ration, and because be himself
is neither sensitive nor intelligent enough to see the larger
picture of his condition (as we do), he manages to convince
himself that there is hope, that his morning "illness" has

been cured. The reader is supposed to know better: Shukhov's evening optimism is a delusion; he fools himself, his ignorance breeds bliss. . . . The purpose of the book is not so much to portray the life of Ivan Denisovich as it is to leave the reader seething with outrage at the murderous injustice of modern Russian life and to make a statement about man's inhumanity to man in the twentieth century. The last thing in the world the novel is really about is one day in the life of one prisoner; the title has a special irony of its own.

An Individual's Story

This approach is not all wrong. We are supposed to see more than Shukhov does. And we would be living in a literary fog if we were to ignore the historical fact that, as Terrence Des Pres puts it, Shukhov's story was "the fate of thousands of Russian prisoners of war [POWs]—the victims of war and the criminal unpreparedness of Russian defenses, of Stalin in particular, the system in general." But the details of Ivan Denisovich's hour-by-hour life matter more than any indictment of the Soviet system which the book provides. Such indictments are commonplace, and some of the best are from Solzhenitsyn's own pen. If we wish to feel pure outrage, *The Gulag Archipelago*, one of the most eloquently angry books ever written, provides us with hundreds of reasons. But *Ivan Denisovich* is about one man, not an entire system. Hence while any responsible reader will pause to ponder the larger political and social and economic forces at work on that one man, he may miss, if he keeps watch only for resounding indictments, the fact that Shukhov, perhaps more than any other character in Solzhenitsyn, is a prime example of life in print.

Shukhov is kept alive partly because Solzhenitsyn conceives him as proceeding step by step, hour by hour, as men alive do. His reactions to the events of his day are interesting and instructive because they are a continuing comment on some rock-hard facts of individual men's lives everywhere, even (especially) for those of us living in comparative luxury, in the West, a world away from the prison camp. We never forget where Shukhov is as we read *Ivan Denisovich*— it is the overwhelming fact of the book—but after only a few pages we should see that the tone and manner of the prose is not soliciting the reader's sympathy so much as his attention, as all deliberately understated prose styles do. The man before us is being squeezed under the excruciating pressure of prison; his life has been stripped to its bare essentials; almost everything has been taken from him. . . .

At the beginning of the novel it is not clear that Shukhov *is* alive or capable of showing us much of anything. He seems dreary and lethargic:

> In his sleep he'd felt very sick and then again a little better.
> All the time he dreaded the morning.
>   But the morning came, as it always did (3).

And then a few lines later: "Shukhov stayed in bed." It is enough to make us wonder if we haven't been here before, but we soon learn that Shukhov really is sick and his back aches (probably a mild case of the flu). Right here, when we first meet him, he is at his lowest point; as soon as he begins to make contact with people, his lethargy will vanish and his attitude will change for the better. Perhaps Solzhenitsyn does intend to hint that even on a day which turns out to be unusually good for Shukhov there are at its beginning faint shadows of despair and hopelessness; one could hardly expect the prisoners to hop out of bed and start singing for joy. Shukhov *would* like to spend the day in bed—what a luxury it would be—and he even tries to arrange it later on.

PRACTICAL WISDOM

But the real Shukhov is no slacker, and he is about as far from being someone in search of himself or of meaning in life as it is possible to be. There is no identity crisis here, no alienation. He knows who he is and where he is, and although this particular morning he is for a time preoccupied with his illness, his mind nevertheless registers his position exactly: "He was lying on the top bunk, with his blanket and overcoat over his head and both his feet tucked in the sleeve of his jacket". . . .

Shukhov knows "what is what in the camps", and he has adjusted himself to the facts of life without being obliterated by that adjustment—not yet, anyway, although he cannot afford to be smug. He wishes to avoid the mess hall job because he knows that he too could become a bowl-licker and destroy the tiny measure of dignity he has left, which he preserves as carefully as fine crystal glass. He knows that there is a point where the needs of the body overwhelm the needs of the spirit, and he wishes to keep clear of that point; once there, the body wins, the spirit loses. . . .

He wishes to do more than survive minimally; he tries to gain an edge when he can, and he is intelligent enough to respect practical wisdom wherever he finds it. He has learned from the past by listening to his elders—in this case, next to a fire in a forest clearing! He has also learned enough on his own to qualify their knowledge somewhat. He has been hardened by eight years in the camps, but he still knows more about people than most of his fellow gang members.

SHUKHOV, A PATHETIC FIGURE?

It is wrong to find the novel the least bit hopeful. In point of fact, *all* Shukhov does is survive, and if at times (such as this one lucky day) he appears to have an edge on the other prisoners, it simply doesn't matter. It is not enough. He is still in prison, and he is likely to die there. His feeble attempts to do battle against his situation are perhaps understandable but are also absurd and pathetic. The possibilities of attainable happiness have been so reduced for Shukhov that we can only shake our heads in dismay. When, for example, the Tartar takes him to the warders' room to mop the floor instead of throwing him in the can and Shukhov is "real pleased" and thanks "the Tartar for letting him off" and when a few minutes later his "pains seemed to have stopped" and he feels "warmer," the reader should see that a life is being wasted here. Nothing at all is being preserved. Shukhov should not have to be grateful to the warder, nor should getting warm in the warders' room be the first good moment of his day (which it is).

But the novel's matter-of-fact tone suggests that both dismay and grand theorizing about the larger wrongs of Shukhov's situation are inappropriate and beside the point. It is as if those things have been done before the book began. Life has already been worse for Shukhov (scurvy, Ust-Izhma, 1943), and he actually regards himself as pretty well off in this camp, a rather endearing attitude; he is a veteran survivor and more. As we watch him plunge his hands into the "steaming bucket" of water and gain some warmth on this frozen morning, we are watching someone intimately acquainted with the necessities of life. Such men are often good instructors. They can remind us of what we need and what we don't—and that can be inspiring. . . .

There are men in the world who can make do with very little, but the scale of the things which can satisfy Shukhov is extraordinarily small—and his (trained) capacity to relish his day's discoveries is extraordinarily large. Over and over

Solzhenitsyn moves the reader directly behind Shukhov as he conducts his mundane affairs, as, for example, when he monitors the warmth of his hands or keeps his eye on the warm spots in camp and at the construction site. Just as we always know how much money people have in a Jane Austen novel, we always know where the stoves are in *Ivan Denisovich* and who is sitting near them. And when Shukhov expresses his pleasure at getting warm (or other achievements of this scale) we are meant to feel with him that at the moment nothing else matters, nothing. We are reminded that even away from the moment, wherever one may be on the planet, maintaining body heat and keeping the fires lit are ancient and fundamentally valuable human tasks. . . .

Shukhov has so little that he knows that exact value of everything he does have; he is a supreme appreciator of his wealth. His world is so barren of objects that he is truly one of those people upon whom nothing is lost. He deserves to have more, but it is also exhilarating to watch him appreciate, just as it must be to watch a starving man eat.

NECESSITY AND LUXURY

Solzhenitsyn makes it perhaps too easy for us to applaud a character's talent for making the best of things. We should not be misled by our enthusiasm. In the above passage (and others like it later on), important discriminations are being made. There are lines drawn in *Ivan Denisovich* between footwear and, say, cigarette butts—the lines between necessity, near necessity, and luxury. . . .

After acquiring boots, he "didn't want to die," thinks Shukhov. The luxury of two pairs does not put him so far out in the sunshine that he becomes silly or thinks he has a bright future, but the two pairs do give him more even than an advantage over others; they give a positive margin of strength. Take one pair away and he still has another. In a step-by-step existence, it is especially nice to be well shod, and he is, and he is proud of it. He has equipped himself for the life at hand, and he has trained himself to think of no other—perhaps that is true wisdom. . . .

Shukhov is a fighter and a winner, but even he is always dangerously close to losing everything he has gained. His is a balancing act. When he has to return the sturdy pair of boots, he loses more than boots: He has retreated backwards, one step closer to a darker place where men want to die, not live. Although he never does fall into that dark place (if someone stole all his boots, he might), much of the tension and excitement in this relatively plotless novel come from our wondering if Shukhov *will* keep his balance. Will he be able to keep on the sunny side of the line? Will he "wangle" enough to maintain his sense of himself as an efficient and alert member of his community?

REFUSING TO STOOP

Not only does Shukhov need a few small victories now and then, but the manner in which he achieves these victories is an issue in *Ivan Denisovich*. Because he knows the ropes and himself so well, because he is so much more fortunate than countless others around him, he also has room enough to keep watch on his own dignity, itself a kind of luxury. One of Shukhov's most interesting small victories (it is called a "great thing") is when he is able to beat out Fetyukov for Caesar's cigarette butt without saying a word.

Shukhov's number (S-854) has just been repainted, and he seems all set for the day. He spots Caesar smoking a cigarette and promptly takes a position next to him, looking past instead of at him. Then Fetyukov arrives and "stood right in front of Caesar and stared with burning eyes at his mouth." Shukhov wants the cigarette ("right now he thought he'd rather have this butt than his freedom"), but he won't "stoop as low as Fetyukov and look straight at the guy's mouth." Shukhov's refusal to stoop is important; he keeps only a blossom of dignity, but it is enough. His need for the cigarette is urgent, he is willing to go pretty far (he "turned halfway" toward Caesar), but he is unwilling to go as far as poor drooling, twitching Fetyukov who finally *asks* Caesar for a drag. In the outside world, the very thought of cadging a butt reveals a beaten man, but here, depending on your manner of receiving it, you can show yourself to be a competent man by accepting one. . . .

One could argue that instead of retaining a measure of "dignity" Shukhov simply knows how to keep from offending others. He is a successful bootlicker who keeps his poise, whereas Fetyukov doesn't know how to conceal his feelings and desires. A truly admirable man would not be trying for Caesar's cigarette butt in the first place. Caesar, after all, toys with *both* Fetyukov and Shukhov. . . .

There are many such moments in *Ivan Denisovich*, moments in which Shukhov becomes eager and obsequious at apparently no cost to himself. Neither are his feelings hurt by Caesar's squeamishness nor are his ("hardened") fingers hurt by the burning cigarette, and in addition he is happy to have beaten poor Fetyukov. In terms of personal dignity, he concedes much here; in return, he gains a cheap sense of victory and a cigarette butt. We know, however, that he is *aware* of everything he does and that while there may be others in camp who would not be so quick to jump after the butt, Shukhov swallows his pride once the butt has been offered—but not before. The line is thin, but it separates the men from the scavengers. . . .

Getting tobacco and cigarettes in *Ivan Denisovich* is not quite the same as getting adequate footwear, but is almost as important: A cigarette means an interval of pure pleasure and satisfaction, a brief captured moment of enjoyment that, unlike eating, you don't absolutely need (although it comes close: "The smoke seemed to go all through his hungry body and into his feet and head"). For men of Shukhov's means, a cigarette is handled as if it were precious metal and is a signal to the reader of how nothing is taken for granted by his class of prisoners.

The urge for a cigarette is a tiny, two-bit, nagging urge which when satisfied in *Ivan Denisovich* reveals how few satisfactions there are in life for these men. At the same time it provides occasion for Solzhenitsyn to show us a man who fully appreciates what is available. At the noon meal break Shukhov manages to borrow some tobacco from Eino:

> Shukhov had some newspaper. He tore a piece off, rolled a cigarette, and lit it with a cinder that had fallen between the boss's feet. And then he dragged and dragged on it, over and over again! He had a giddy feeling all over his body, like it was going to his feet as well as his head.

Rarely has a cigarette been so enjoyed in literature.

Shukhov's manner of achieving this small victory is exemplary. In order to get that cigarette, he has had to assure Eino of his reliability ("You know I won't gyp you"). Eino has to check with his close friend ("They always shared and shared alike and wouldn't use a single shred of tobacco without the other knowing"); Eino then measures out enough for one cigarette. It is a precise and careful transaction which involves not only a valuable commodity but Shukhov's integrity—*and* the bond of friendship between

Eino and his pal. Like a bullfight in Hemingway, there is a proper way to conduct this transaction; more than a single cigarette is at stake. Shukhov manages to keep his poise; Fetyukov loses his. . . .

Shukhov is distracted here by an ethical question which seems to arise whenever he has more than he "needs." The small margin he so often gains on this day he can certainly appreciate, but he cannot revel in it. He deserves an interval of pure, unalloyed self-indulgence, but something in him won't allow it. (In fact, though no saint, he has a conscience.) Shukhov's acquisition of wealth (a whole cigarette, not just a butt) automatically triggers two questions: Should I share it? With whom? So despite the repeated statement in *Ivan Denisovich* that in prison it is dog-eat-dog and every-man-for-himself, only a heartless person can enjoy his hard-earned cigarette (or extra gruel, or cookies) without its becoming a moral and ethical issue.

MAKING JUDGMENTS

Shukhov pities Senka Klevshin because he is deaf, because he is not pushy like Fetyukov, and because he had been in Buchenwald. Fetyukov was only a factory manager; Senka's credentials are far more impressive, and Shukhov finds him worthy of the cigarette butt. In the space of only a few lines, what begins as a simple action—one man trying to enjoy a cigarette—becomes a moral issue. When Shukhov chooses Senka over Fetyukov as the rightful heir to the cigarette butt, he is making a judgment of the sort which occurs everywhere in Solzhenitsyn's work.

In one way or another Shukhov judges everyone he meets. We are also meant to judge everyone Shukhov meets, as well as Shukhov himself, and by the end of the novel, as in all Solzhenitsyn's works, we should be able to say exactly where every character fits on a carefully calibrated moral scale. Shukhov does not make a show of moral judgments, nor does he agonize over them, nor would he call himself a judge or a moralist or even a man on the lookout for kindness (though he is). . . . Shukhov is basically a good man (or at least a man with good in him), but the prison does not allow him to be as good as he could be. He talks tougher than he feels, which is often the way of men under pressure.

One of the things that makes Solzhenitsyn unusual among contemporary writers is his refusal to regard good and evil as outdated, either as words or concepts. Judging a particular action as right or wrong is not merely a matter of one's point of view; a reliable and absolute guide to morality exists. But in *Ivan Denisovich*, where does it come from? God? The Russian Church? An inner light? Peasant wisdom? Solzhenitsyn himself does not seem sure, not in *Ivan Denisovich*—and I say this even though today it is common knowledge that Solzhenitsyn is emphatically a Christian and even though his later work emphatically clarifies the sources of his moral position. Sources aside for the time being, the moral standard in this novel is as real as cigarettes and boots, though some characters cannot see it and would deny it if they could see it. As Shukhov proceeds step by step through the day, his mind alert and his eyes as sharp as an eagle's, he is not purposely conducting an inquiry into human behavior, yet he registers every nuance of kindness, every tiny sliver of hate and injustice.

Work as Redemption

Olivier Clément

In the novel, Shukhov is always engaged in manual labor—bending pipes, laying bricks, carrying mortar, leveling a wall—to the point of fatigue and exhaustion. Author Olivier Clément, a professor of Slavic literature, points out that Shukhov's work restores his vitality. Clément likens Shukhov's activities to the Christian process of self-emptying that accompanies spiritual awakening. Through work, the inmates are united by a sense of accomplishment and by the pursuit of a common goal.

The first lesson that Solzhenitsyn draws from his long experience of the camps, his long association with the oppressed from every walk of life, is that political, economic, and social alienation does not fundamentally affect the nature of work. . . . The most remarkable descriptions the author has given us of man at work refer to a prison camp in Kazakhstan, the camp of Ivan Denisovich. (*One Day in the Life of Ivan Denisovich* is nonetheless concerned with a good day in the life of a man accustomed to manual work. In many camps the work, exceeding a man's strength, would destroy him, and the prisoner could only respond with hatred, despair and duplicity.) Thus social exclusion and economic servitude in no way prejudice the ontological reality of work in so far as it is carried through by persons and is linked with the awakening of personal awareness; which is not the case when man "becomes a beast", trampling mercilessly on others in order to survive. . . .

Work, like the awareness it can express, is something more than the economic and social context in which it goes on. But what is it?

A CALMING DISCIPLINE

Solzhenitsyn replies that work is first of all a purifying discipline, an approach to awareness by way of the body. In one

Reprinted by permission of Burns & Oates, an imprint of Continuum International Publishers, from *The Spirit of Solzhenitsyn*, by Olivier Clément.

respect this is the traditional Christian attitude: the Fathers of the Church in no way regarded work as a curse, but first and foremost as the "absorber of iniquity", and ascetics know from experience how the most repetitive manual work can provide favourable conditions for concentration. . . .

One of the reasons for the calming effect of work lies in the repeated gesture, in so far as it produces a rhythm which becomes one with the principal rhythms of the body, encouraging them and bringing them to the level of consciousness. . . .

Work, by the very fatigue it causes, activates, amplifies and enhances the breathing and deep-seated physical energies and draws attention to the healthy warmth of one's blood. The progressive onset of "waves of heat" is particularly noticeable in very cold weather, as Solzhenitsyn remarks apropos of Ivan Denisovich and his companions: "Thanks to the urgent work, the first wave of heat had come over them—when you feel wet under your coat . . . And after about an hour they had their second flush of heat, the one that dries up the sweat. Their feet didn't feel cold. . .".

For most of our contemporaries in 'technopolis' these energies remain dormant; they are familiar with nervous exhaustion, not with the deep, healthy fatigue through which man restores his vitality. Now, the mobilization of these deep-seated physical energies is related to the search for what the ascetics of the Orthodox Church called "the seat of the heart": when man enters into a dialogue with matter, whether directly, in nature, or in things made by others, the correlation between thought and gesture, the incarnation of thought in manual terms, awakens that center of unity which the same tradition describes as the union of mind and heart. The man who has banished all extraneous thoughts from his mind is able to concentrate on a single idea and to *make* that idea, not by arbitrarily imposing it on matter, but by yielding to the latter in order to give expression to its structure and dynamism. So it is for Ivan Denisovich when, on a construction site, he works hard, to improvise a heating system, joining and bending the pipes that are to get rid of the smoke. The flow of associated thoughts impinging on the mind, time divided between nostalgic regret and worry about the future, and finally its absence, all this disappears when, in order to be realized in matter, an idea must recognize and take into account the possibilities of the latter, not just intellectually, but through the mediating incarnation of bodily gesture: here it is a question of joining metal cylinders, the diameters of which are not exactly identical, of capturing and channeling the elusive movement of the smoke. There is the fact of the smoke, the recalcitrance of the ill-assorted pipes, and, the need for a smokeless heat which will make survival and work possible in spite of the severe cold of the steppe. This may be a point of detail, but it requires the collaboration of several people in a vast dialogue between men, things and nature which, at the point where personal intelligence, the world and the body meet, facilitates the development of awareness.

CREATING TOGETHER

These characteristics are found and others emerge when the task in hand is truly the work of a team. Creative joy is born, not in spite of hardship and fatigue, nor by suppressing them, but through them, according to that pattern of self-emptying and self-transcendence which, in Solzhenitsyn, always accompanies a spiritual awakening. Once, Ivan Denisovich and his team-mates have organized a rudimentary stove near which the mortar can be prepared; they must set about constructing a wall out of stone blocks. The conditions of work themselves call for speed: the cold freezes the mortar within a few seconds, making it set too quickly, and if a block has not been put in the right place there is no time to try again or put it right, and the plumb is lost; if there is too much mortar the whole thing will begin to slip and will collapse when the thaw comes. To the need for speed is added the resistance, the hostility even, of the material and milieu: the cold bites and can even paralyze one, the blocks are sharp and one risks tearing one's mittens. What is more, the blocks are far from being uniform; they have "chipped corners or broken edges or lumps on their sides"; the geometrical and industrially produced object thus rediscovers something of the character of its natural material—stone.

The work can only be carried out therefore through a synchronization of thought and action. There must be "vision" which must in turn be translated almost immediately into action. Ivan "sees", "at first glance", the individual character of each block, its peculiar irregularity, and at the same time he "sees" the place that corresponds to it in the wall. He takes the steaming mortar on his trowel, measuring the exact amount needed to fix the block horizontally, and to join two contiguous blocks, bearing in mind that this join will be supporting the middle of a block on the next row up. Next, before the mortar has a chance to freeze, but with sufficient care to protect his mitten, he grabs the chosen block, "and without losing a moment he levels it, patting it with the side of the trowel", for "the mortar is already freezing". The rigours of the climate and a hard-won expertise combine to produce a light, rhythmic, almost dance-like discipline, and man arranges matter according to the beautiful geometry it demands, in a play of alternating movements which conquers gravity by making use of it.

GIVES BIRTH TO BROTHERHOOD

The rhythm is communicated to the whole team; as a result of the synchronized movements a wonderful relationship is established between the men, and finally between the stretches of wall that grow and connect with one another. Apart from brief appeals to the mortar-carriers, words are useless: everything goes so quickly that there is not even time to wipe one's nose. But there are signs of communication: Senka, who lays the blocks on one side, and Ivan, who lays them on the other, both on the same level, meet one another and begin to scoop mortar out of the same hod. The team, reflects Ivan Denisovich, is a family, and matter sets the seal on the brotherhood of the men in so far as the men seal the elements of matter together in some kind of order. Even with the team leader, whom he has learnt to respect, Ivan now feels on an equal footing: "Now, after working like that, he felt equal to the team leader". . . .

These examples show what manual work—which involves the whole man—means to Solzhenitsyn, and it is a far cry from the utopias of "creativity" and play which would like to forget that the mastery of anything requires a hard apprenticeship and daily practice, and that exultation of the creative moment comes at the end of a long process of development. It is a far cry, too, from the piecemeal, totally unstimulating work of so many modem factories where man is subjected to mechanical cadences which scarcely ever fall into a rhythm to synchronize with the rhythms of the body. The primitive equipment of the workers described by Solzhenitsyn, their need to get on with the job in spite of everything, paradoxically enough lends a freedom to their movements that many "free" workers do not possess. . . . several skills, and should feel sufficiently responsible as one of a team that is itself responsible. Some attempt is being made today in the industrialized countries, radically to modify conditions of work, and here Solzhenitsyn's concept of work as inseparable from spiritual awareness and the capacity to "think with one's hands", as a dialogue with people and things through the medium of matter, could be very helpful —on condition that the primacy passes from the project of work to the man who works.

THE AWAKENING OF CONSCIENCE

Nothing fruitful can be achieved therefore in any domain whatsoever by someone who is not spiritually aware. If he wants to educate or heal others as whole beings he must strive first to unify himself; he must "think with his hands" until he acquires that mastery which sets him free for laughter and from the weight of time. At the end of the day when Ivan Denisovich and the team leader share a good laugh, Ivan exclaims: "Why do these rats make the work-day so short? We're just getting into our stride when they call it off". If respect for man is one manifestation of spiritual awareness, so is respect for matter and the efforts of others. In Ivan's work teams that day they overestimate the quantity of mortar, and a boxful still remains when it is time to go. To leave it would simply be to waste both contents and container: "Next morning they could throw the whole lot of it to hell—the mortar would have petrified, it wouldn't yield to a pick-axe". The team leader accepts the situation with reluctance—the more so because it would be dangerous to arrive late at the various control points separating the work yard from the camp. "But Shukhov wasn't made that way: eight years in a camp couldn't change his nature. He worried about anything he could make use of, about every scrap of work he could do". In any case his energy and creative enthusiasm are such that he cannot simply shut off like a machine, so he stays there alone, at his own risk, to go one with the wall until the mortar is used up. . . .

TRUE ART

The genuine work of art is neither an ideological drum nor the gold tracery that has nothing behind it. It is, Solzhenitsyn tells is, "true", and the word needs to be examined. The truth of which Solzhenitsyn speaks, and which, as we shall see, is truth-justice, is radically different from ideology. It signifies the reality of people and things—their mystery, which can be reduced neither to conceptual form in a system nor to objective *praxis*. In *One Day in the Life of Ivan Denisovich* Tzezar Markovich, the film director agreeably relaxed, engages in a conversation on art with a prisoner, X123, who happens to pass through his office, and of whom we know nothing except that he is "a stringy old man . . . serving a twenty year sentence". Apropos of the film *Ivan the Terrible* Tzezar praises the genius of Sergey Eisenstein. The old man's response is uncompromising. On the one hand, he says, "it's all so arty there's no art left in it"—full of a self-conscious aestheticism, while true beauty is, to use Plato's phrase, nothing more or less than the "splendour of truth". Beauty is bread for the heart, but the aesthete forgets the bread of being and serves up nothing but a borrowed, violent beauty—"spice and poppy-seed instead of everyday bread and butter". Beauty such as this is cut off from the true and the good; it can get on quite happily with ideological falsehood and political oppression. *Ivan the Terrible* attempts "the justification of personal tyranny". Tzezar's answer to this is that art is not a question of content but of form, not of "*what* but *how*". X123 explodes: "To bloody hell with your *how* if it doesn't arouse any good feelings in me". It would be over-hasty and inexact to assume from this that the anonymous old man is one of the last surviving members of the sectarian and moralizing intelligentsia. He is a witness whom a tragic history has brought back to what is essential, to "the one thing necessary". By "good feeling" he, like Solzhenitsyn himself, means that openness to being, that ontological goodness in which the person is fulfilled in the truth of love.

The notion of goodness has great significance in countries that have been influenced by the "spiritual sensitivity" of Orthodox Christianity. Firstly, because eastern Christianity remains, to some extent, an interiorized form of Hellenism, and has therefore inherited (although it transposes it by means of a different combination) the ancient equation of the *kalos k'agathos*, the beautiful and the good, in the sense of a craftsmanlike (and disciplined), heroic (and sanctifying) shaping of the whole man. Secondly, and above all, because man, according to the mystical theology of the eastern Church, is called to share in the "divine energies" which are so many aspects of the Presence. Now, each "virtue" signifies a share in one of the divine names—in a divine energy— and goodness manifests both ontological fulness and personal communion. It is inseparable from beauty, because the fulfilment of being in love allows the Light to shine forth. Authentic art—and this is surely true of Solzhenitsyn's— thus enables us to sense the holiness of being in the truth of persons. . . .

In his autobiographical notes Solzhenitsyn stresses that "the writer's obligations to the individual person are no less than those he has towards society". Or rather, it is when he starts from the person as a unique, irreducible expression of the biological and social whole that the writer can really understand and serve society. Only thus does he avoid the lies of the "hirelings" and the temptation to retreat "into worlds of his own creation or the wastes of subjective caprice"; and so discover the seeds and roots of social phenomena, warding off or denouncing everything in these meta-historical depths that seems to him "unhealthy and disturbing". The great artist is a visionary, not in the romantic but in the prophetic sense of "discerner of spirits". Moreover, the artist, like the prophet, expresses far more through his art than he knows or imagines he is doing. For although his thoughts, more often than not, spring from his own inner world, his creative activity begins in that luminous darkness where he is separated from no one.

In this way the true creator senses in the "heart" of man the orientations, attitudes and choices that will make the history of tomorrow. Fyodor Dostoevsky, observes Solzhenitsyn, brought to light the demonic forces that were to be unleashed in the nihilism of the twentieth century, and other examples come to mind: long before the First World War or the concentration camps, Franz Kafka and Pablo Picasso described a world of suspicion and torture, the destruction of individuality, the "death of man". And yet, reading *The Brothers Karamazov*, Boris Pasternak's *Doctor Zhivago*, or the novels of Solzhenitsyn, one becomes aware of the forces that are being mustered in secret by the powers of good and who tomorrow perhaps, a "cloud of witnesses", will shine out in the history of our time.

One Day, a Modern Epic

Robert Porter

Robert Porter, who teaches Russian at the University of Bristol, contends that critics who consider the novel mainly as an exposé of a corrupt system fail to see the work's universality, which is its greater asset. Porter likens the novel, with its array of characters with distinct personalities and idiosyncrasies, to a modern epic. Porter concludes that *One Day* triumphs, most of all, as a subversion of the materialist philosophy.

When *One Day in the Life of Ivan Denisovich* appeared in 1962 it produced an extraordinary range of responses. Ex-prisoners commented on the authenticity of what Solzhenitsyn described, while some die-hard Stalinists were outraged by the author's negative portrayal of Soviet life. The mainstream reviewers, broadly speaking, saw the work as a necessary exercise in exorcism, so that the Soviet system might continue on its path of democratization under Khrushchev. While it is right and proper to read the work primarily as an exposé of Stalin's crimes, to leave it at that would be to rank Solzhenitsyn as no more than a highly competent journalist. *One Day in the Life of Ivan Denisovich*'s literary qualities have moved generations of readers from all round the world, and its special features endow the work with a universality that rises above political demarcation lines.

We follow Ivan Denisovich Shukhov throughout the day from reveille at 5 o'clock to lights out, from his bunk, to the guard-house floor he has to wash, to the mess-hall, the sick-bay, then as he is marched out of the camp for the day's work, his return, the evening meal, and excursion to a neighboring barracks hut to buy tobacco and then back to his own hut. Much of the story is told in an adapted form of *skaz*, whereby the narrator reports Ivan's thought processes

From "*One Day in the Life of Ivan Denisovich*," by Robert Porter, in *Reference Guide to Russian Literature*, edited by Neil Cornwell (Chicago: Fitzroy Dearborn, 1998). Reprinted by permission of the publisher.

and perceptions in his own peasant speech, while occasionally employing a more neutral, "omniscient narrator" tone and viewpoint. Solzhenitsyn was most keen that his hero should be an uneducated peasant, unable to verbalize fully, let alone rationalize, his predicament. Thus he comes across as a thoroughly credible type, not like the somewhat contrived peasant philosophers that Tolstoi sometimes produced.

DISTINCT INDIVIDUALITY

There is a strong Tolstoian element in the work, though. With an economical use of formal description and snatches of dialogue, the author creates a vast array of characters, all with their idiosyncrasies, despite the dehumanizing conformity of their lives: guards and prisoners alike are slaves to routine and they all wear uniforms. Naturally the prisoners are most subject to uniformity, but even here the wayward human spirit breaks through, bestowing a degree of individuality and dignity: "Fetiukov was one of the lowliest members of the gang—even Shukhov was a cut above him. Outwardly the gang all looked the same but there were big differences." Ivan is slightly amused by the heroic protest of Buinovsky when the prisoners are made to undo their shirts to be searched, a futile gesture that earns the former sea captain ten days in the punishment cell. Ivan, by contrast, is much more resourceful and experienced, never missing an opportunity, for example, to earn an extra scrap of food from the better-off prisoners who might receive food parcels. He starts the day badly, feeling unwell and unable to be placed on the sick list, but he grows in mind and body as the hours pass, so that by the afternoon and early evening he is working flat out on the brick-laying to which he has been assigned. His motivation at this point has nothing to do with any a priori material considerations, and in the closing sentences of the story he recalls the enjoyment he found in his work. Elsewhere too, we see that the human impulse springs not always from the quest for material survival: "He ate every bit of every fish, gills, tails, even eyes if they were where they should be, but if they had boiled out of the head and were floating loose in the bowl—big fish-eyes goggling at him—he wouldn't eat them. The others laughed at him for it." In Ivan's survival and in the impression the reader has of a vast and self-contained world—which is both temporal and geographical—there is something of the epic.

Ivan has memories of his life on the collective farm before

the war and he is unable to comprehend what his wife tells him in her twice-yearly letters, for instance about some of the peasants now making healthy sums of money by stencilling patterns on cheap material to sell as carpets. The hero is more superstitious than religious, telling Buinovsky that in his village the peasants believed that God broke up the moon each month to make stars. There are more unequivocal illustrations of religious devotion, notably in the figure of Alyrsha, the Baptist. Ivan is unable to relate to the world of intellectuals, and indeed intellectuals do not take notice of him; witness the scene where he takes Tsezar's dinner to him and overhears the latter's argument with Kh-123 about Sergey Eisenstein. None of the characters finds himself where he truly belongs, and in this, *One Day in the Life of Ivan Denisovich* is about dislocation and alienation.

For a work that aspires through flesh and blood characters to epic proportions, the text has a curious modernist flavour to it, seeking as it does to establish an entire universe within the parameters of one day and one psyche. Here is a world in which nearly all actions are explained and yet one that has no overall *raison d'être*—there is only one oblique reference to Stalin, and the charges brought against the various prisoners are spurious in the extreme. Foreign critics were quick to see the labor camp as a microcosm of Soviet society as a whole. Max Hayward went further, seeing the work as a comment on modern man in general and arguing that in it the Kafkaesque nightmare had become the reality. Certainly, the world that Ivan Denisovich accepts so matter-of-factly ("almost a happy day" the hero reflects at the end) leaves the reader disorientated and outraged. The mixture of dialect, prison slang, and obscenity—such a contrast to the prudish Sovietese of the time—plays no small part in the shock tactics. However, some subtler devices are at work too, not least in the references to the natural elements, which, despite their harshness, provide a link to a more normal world: at times even this natural order seems threatened, as when the camp searchlights make the stars look dim; yet at other times the natural world provides, irrationally, spiritual sustenance: "Aleshka gazed at the sun and a happy smile spread from his eyes to his lips . . . what had he got to be happy about?" *One Day in the Life of Ivan Denisovich* describes the horrors of labor-camp life, but ultimately it is more subversive in its quiet dismissal of materialist philosophy.

CHAPTER 2

The Character of Ivan Denisovich Shukhov

Shukhov Is Vital to Understanding Solzhenitsyn

Edward E. Ericson Jr.

Although *One Day* is often read as a political statement, Edward E. Ericson Jr. argues that its appeal is a moral one. The novel is not so much a portrayal of a Stalinist concentration camp, but a delineation of man's inhumanity to man. What allows Shukhov to endure in the face of cruelty and corruption is his humanity—his attempt to maintain a balance between his needs and those of his fellow prisoners. Ericson further asserts that Shukhov and Alyosha embody the best of human qualities: generosity and faith in spite of the deprivation of prison life. Ericson is a professor of English at Calvin College in Grand Rapids, Michigan.

The story of the publication of *One Day in the Life of Ivan Denisovich* is one of the exciting literary stories of our time. When, in 1961, Solzhenitsyn hoped that the Soviet cultural climate might possibly have thawed enough to allow his novel to be published, he sought to get it through to Alexander Tvardovsky, editor of *Novy Mir....*

Tvardovsky, the supreme literary diplomat, using his powerful position and connections, went right to the top and sought from Nikita Khrushchev permission to publish the novel. Khrushchev apparently decided that this novel would help him consolidate his base of power, which he was building partly on a denunciation of Stalin's corruption of total control. Khrushchev's fellow members of the Politburo felt that they had little choice but to allow *Novy Mir* to publish the controversial novel.

It appeared in the November 1962 issue, in an overrun of ninety-five thousand which sold out immediately. A separate run of nearly a million copies also sold out quickly. An unknown small-town teacher was, at one stroke, on the center stage of Russian literature. The whole world took note. For his "liberalism" Khrushchev was praised widely.

PLUNGED INTO POLITICS

Early reviews, even in the most orthodox of Soviet sources, were overwhelmingly favorable. *Pravda* [official newspaper of the Communist Party] remarked on Solzhenitsyn's "profound humanity, because people remained people even in an atmosphere of mockery." Zhores Medvedev, who was later to write *Ten Years after Ivan Denisovich*, emphasized the artistry of the novel. But most responses, in keeping with Khrushchev's motivation for allowing publication, centered on the book's political significance. Importantly, most Western reviews also emphasized the political dimension; the book's publication was viewed as an event illustrating the increasing thaw within the Soviet Union, thus auguring well for future East-West relations. So from the beginning Solzhenitsyn's work was viewed through the wrong lens.

A political approach does not penetrate to the heart of *One Day*. The novel is not, in its essence, about Stalin's inhumanity to man; it is about man's inhumanity to man. Stalin is not some aberration in an otherwise smooth progression of humaneness in history. The evil of the human heart is a universal theme: this is Solzhenitsyn's approach.

Perhaps never has the political appropriation of a work of art by state authorities backfired so dramatically and totally as in the case of *One Day*. Once having been catapulted into the limelight of world attention, Solzhenitsyn would not be silent. Now he had a platform, and his sense of duty urged him on. Khrushchev had let out of the bottle a genie which his successors could not put back in. The high visibility afforded by Khrushchev's decision provided Solzhenitsyn with all the protection of world opinion which he needed in order to escape the brutalities which almost certainly would otherwise have been visited upon him for saying what he went on to say. . . .

FOCUS ON IVAN

The novel depicts a single day in the life of a simple peasant, Ivan Denisovich Shukhov, who has been unjustly thrown into a prison camp. While we see many of his fellow *zeks* [prisoners], the focus remains rather tightly fixed on

Shukhov. It is a day in which not much, certainly nothing momentous, happens. The *zeks* [prisoners] eat their pitifully inadequate gruel, work hard as bricklayers and foundrymen (Solzhenitsyn himself worked as both), are counted and re-counted, and finally retire—to prepare for another day, and other days, of the same.

Solzhenitsyn shows great respect for his title character. Shukhov is not at all an authorial alter ego, as are Oleg Kostoglotov in *Cancer Ward* (somewhat) and Gleb Nerzhin in *The First Circle* (considerably). The clearest sign of respect is in the mere naming of the hero, The combination of given name (Ivan—significantly, the most common of Russian names) and patronymic (Denisovich—sort of Denis) is a polite form most readily used for persons of high station or intrinsic importance. Solzhenitsyn applies it to a simple peasant. The author deems his character worthy of the respect usually reserved for "important" people.

The most memorable technical trait of *One Day* is its understatement. The novel depicts horrors which might well elicit white-hot anger—or, if not that, a kind of sentimentality over the suffering of innocents. The novel makes no such explicit claim on our emotions. Rather, it describes the day of Shukhov and his fellows as not too bad, as almost a good day. The final passage of the novel, capped by a brilliantly conceived final sentence, highlights the device of understatement:

> Shukhov went to sleep, and he was very happy. He'd had a lot of luck today. They hadn't put him in the cooler. The gang hadn't been chased out to work in the Socialist Community Development. He'd finagled an extra bowl of mush at noon. The boss had gotten them good rates for their work. He'd felt good making that wall. They hadn't found that piece of steel in the frisk. Caesar had paid him off in the evening, He'd bought some tobacco. And he'd gotten over that sickness.
>
> Nothing had spoiled the day and it had been almost happy.
>
> There were three thousand six hundred and fifty-three days like this in his sentence, from reveille to lights out.
>
> The extra ones were because of the leap years. . . .

This concluding passage also allows us to check on the important technical matter of narrative point of view. It is a matter handled delicately but consistently in this novel. The author is always telling the story; Shukhov is always in the third person. Yet, by a clever sleight of hand, the author keeps making his readers feel as if they are inside the mind of the main character; truly, Ivan Denisovich is the one who thinks that this is not the worst of days. Readers are left with the impression that they see and experience Shukhov's day through his own eyes, though in technical fact they never do. In this, Solzhenitsyn has shown considerable skill as a fiction writer.

SUFFERING IS BOTH PHYSICAL AND METAPHYSICAL

As is typical of Solzhenitsyn's works, *One Day* shows us suffering humanity *in extremis*. But because of Shukhov's limited perspective, suffering here is depicted as primarily physical. In *The First Circle* the more sophisticated Gleb Nerzhin shows that suffering is also psychological and even spiritual. Yet both of these novels—in contrast with *Cancer Ward*, which deals with the *mystery* of suffering—treat a suffering the perpetrator of which is no mystery at all. Still, even in *One Day* the suffering of the body takes on a metaphysical dimension—through the mediation of the author, who can go beyond the ken of the main character. The inhospitably cold climate becomes a symbol of the inhumane setting for human life in general, and the reader comes away feeling moral outrage rather than mere vicarious physical pain. When a medical assistant finds the feverish Ivan not ill enough to exempt from the day's work, the author queries, "How can you expect a man who's warm to understand a man who's cold?" It is one of those microcosmic remarks from which ray out large symbolic meanings. The warm man is the one open to perpetrating injustice. Solzhenitsyn devotes his life to making warm men feel the cold.

Any such "big" thoughts are as far beyond Shukhov as they are beyond the prison guards. Shukhov, now yearning after a handful of oats that once he would have fed only to his horses, thinks, as he gets his pittance of food for the day, "This was what a prisoner lived for, this one little moment." But even here the stomach is cheated and the soul, thereby, troubled. And what do these guards of the "animals" care? "Every ration was short. The only question was—by how much? So you checked every day to set your mind at rest, hoping you hadn't been too badly treated."

The arbitrariness of the life of the zeks is all-governing. The guards are not allowed to recognize the diversity and unpredictability of life; only two zeks may be sick per day; only two letters per zek may be mailed out per year. "Soviet power," Solzhenitsyn satirizes, has decreed that the sun stands highest in the sky not at noon but an hour later. Being dehumanized entails being denatured.

Given the collectivist ideology of the Soviets, an ironic effect of their prison regimen is that it breaks down the sense of human solidarity. Solzhenitsyn, who speaks consistently on behalf of individual dignity, always speaks with equal consistency on behalf of human solidarity. So he laments that in a zek's mind it is another zek who is one's worst enemy. Occasional displays of solidarity, which should be a natural outflowing of the zeks' common humanity and their shared plight, usually succumb to the camp attitude, "You croak today but I mean to live till tomorrow."

Nevertheless, however much the grim environment and the need to adapt somehow to it may reduce the basic humanity of the zeks, such pressures can never eradicate the human essence. To be sure, Shukhov is constantly and instinctively concerned with self-preservation. When he was accused, absurdly, of high treason for surrendering to the Germans with the intention of betraying his country, he coolly calculated: "If he didn't sign, he was as good as buried. But if he did, he'd still go on living a while. So he signed." But there is more. A man will assert his wants as well as his needs. For instance, he wants to smoke; it is an unnecessary small pleasure, but he will find a way. Then, there is satisfaction in work. Ivan works poorly only when given meaningless tasks. Laying bricks well pleases him, even if in prison. Constructive work brings out in him the ennobling quality of self-validation through creative effort. . . .

MAN ENDURES

The greatest of all human capacities demonstrated by Ivan Denisovich is his capacity to absorb pain and yet to endure with at least some vestiges of humanity intact. This enduring humanity is one of Solzhenitsyn's most important themes, and it is his great consolation as he weeps for mankind. The best efforts to reduce humanity to the level of the animal are never entirely successful; and, by definition, a process of dehumanization which is not totally successful is a failure: some humanity remains. "There's nothing you can't do to a man . . ."—except that you cannot do away with his humanity altogether. Longsuffering, Solzhenitsyn thinks, is a peculiarly strong trait of the Russian peasantry. The peasant may be patient, but he is also durable; and ultimately he will overcome.

Ivan Denisovich's attitude toward religion is much like Matryona's in "Matryona's House." Both show little interest in formal religion, either ecclesiastical or credal. Yet both breathe a kind of natural piety, and religious references pepper their everyday talk. Ivan's ready response to his tribulations in prison is, "As long as you're in the barracks—praise the Lord and sit tight." At day's end, grateful that he is not in the cells and thinking that it is not "so bad sleeping here," he murmurs, "Thank God." When he forgets until the last moment before he is frisked that he has a hacksaw blade on him, he almost involuntarily prays as "hard as he could": "God in Heaven, help me and keep me out of the can!" Afterwards, however, this down-to-earth peasant "didn't say a prayer of thanks because there wasn't any time and there was no sense in it now."

Ivan's faith is naive and unreasoned, and includes a sizeable dose of superstition. He believes in God: "When He thunders up there in the sky, how can you help believe in Him?" He also believes, as folk in his village do, that each month God makes a new moon, because he needs the old one to crumble up into stars: "The stars keep falling down, so you've got to have new ones in their place." Atheistic rulers may curtail the growth of religion ("The Russians didn't even remember which hand you cross yourself with"), but it is beyond their power to shake the faith of the Matryonas and Ivans.

IVAN'S HOPE, ALYOSHA'S FAITH

While Solzhenitsyn clearly admires Ivan's faith, Ivan does not represent his religious ideal. A character who comes closer to doing so is Alyosha (or Alyoshka) the Baptist. . . . Solzhenitsyn's handling of Alyosha shows that his primary religious concerns are not with the particularities of Orthodoxy but with those central aspects of the Christian faith held in common by all Christians.

The climactic conversation of the novel is between Ivan and Alyosha. Alyosha's prominence here has been prepared for by frequent earlier depictions of him as a good worker and kind person. Alyosha's faith does not incapacitate him for survival. On the contrary, it is a source of the inner strength that so often characterizes Solzhenitsyn's little heroes, the small people who somehow are able to withstand everything that a soulless bureaucracy inflicts on them. . . .

Alyosha scolds Ivan for not praying "hard enough," and adds, "if you have faith and tell the mountain to move, it will move." This bold confidence is too much for literal-minded Ivan, who has never seen a mountain move (though he then allows that he has never seen a mountain at all!). For his part, Ivan, unlike those zeks who have lost their capacity for compassion, pities the Baptists as "poor fellows": They were in no one's way, and "all they did was pray to God"; yet "they all got twenty-five years . . . ." On the question of mountain-moving, Alyosha asserts the supremacy of the spiritual realm over the material, since of all physical things, the Lord commanded them to pray only for their daily bread; beyond that, "We must pray about things of the spirit—that the Lord Jesus should remove the scum of anger from our hearts. . . ."

Ivan does not want to be misunderstood. Although disillusioned by a bad priest, he insists that he believes in God. "But what I don't believe in is Heaven and Hell." The afterlife, after all, is not open to empirical verification, as are monthly new moons and falling stars. When he prays, he says, it will be for something real, like release from prison. This attitude scandalizes Alyosha, who consciously suffers for Christ. He counters, "What do you want your freedom for? What faith you have left will be choked in thorns. Rejoice that you are in prison. Here you can think of your soul." This spiritual focus, which Solzhenitsyn elsewhere asserts in his own person, affects Ivan: "Alyosha was talking the truth. You could tell by his voice and his eyes he was glad to be in prison.". . .

Although he cannot believe everything Alyosha can, Ivan's actions are as good as anyone's. Considering Alyosha impractical, always giving and never getting, Ivan gives him a biscuit, though that gesture leaves the giver with nothing for himself. Solzhenitsyn comments, "We've nothing but we always find a way to make something extra." Ivan gives the cup of cold water, though not always knowingly in God's name. If Alyosha has the best words, no one has better deeds than Ivan.

Ivan and Alyosha are brothers under the skin. Both are models of humanity in the midst of inhumanity; both care for others as much as for themselves. Ivan represents the best possible from a man without an articulated faith; a man can act very well without faith in a transcendent reality. Such a one is in no position, however, to explain the mystery of suffering. This crucial matter, which Ivan deeply needs, is what Alyosha can add. Without Alyosha, the novel would be much diminished. Ivan, as good as he is, needs Alyosha's insight to complete the picture.

Shukhov, the Quintessential Survivor

Terrence Des Pres

Terrence Des Pres, French scholar and author, considers Shukhov as the epitome of the survivor. He argues that when confronted with extremity—a situation that tests the limits of human endurance—a survivor will refuse to acknowledge that condition and will devise ways to actually transcend the experience. Des Pres points to two images that demonstrate Shukhov's survival ethic: taking great satisfaction in having done a good job building the prison wall and relishing the taste and nourishment of a thin, meager soup. As a result of his will-power, Shukhov succeeds at subverting the "anti-world" of prison and expanding his own life force. At the time of writing, Des Pres was Junior Fellow in the Harvard Society of Fellows and holder of the Crawshaw Chair in English literature at Colgate University.

The definite characteristic of the survivor is that he survives not in body only, but also in spirit, enduring anti-human conditions without the loss of his will to carry on in human ways. Alexander Solzhenitsyn is a great example, a man of tried humanity who survived the Russian front, eight years in Stalin's camps, cancer, and for many years the suppression of his identity as a Russian writer. But to make of this brave man an object of examination would be to mythicise him, to remove him from the unique density of fact and contingency which is the life of the individual in history as opposed to the timeless image of the hero. Myth cannot be escaped, in which case it seems better to deal directly with fiction. . . .

From "The Survivor: On the Ethos of Survival in Extremity," by Terrence Des Pres, *Encounter*, vol. 37, no. 3, September 1971. Copyright © 1971 by Terrence Des Pres. Reprinted by permission of Georges Borchardt, Inc., for the author.

KEEPING FAITH

This kind of extremity requires an attitude which will allow men to act, to keep faith in themselves and thereby to move beyond their fate as victims. First of all, then, the survivor is not a victim merely. He is the victim who refuses to accept his victimisation as total, who fights it as best he can, and who will not, either by act or attitude, consent to the death of himself or anyone else. He will not, that is, accept the logic of the situation imposed upon him.

Dehumanisation and death are the results of extremity, and they may appear to cynicism and common sense alike as reasonable, or even inevitable, consequences. Prolonged and encompassing, the forces of negation may seem to *be* reality. But the survivor holds life and spirit within himself and knows, by the plain fact that he exists, a greater reality. He clings to his faith in the value and dignity of living things, and will not bow to destruction. So long as there is a way, his will is active in rebellion against the anti-world. He will overthrow it if he can, but in any case, by the fact that he exists, he rejects its law. . . .

Survival, as defined in this article, is an act of refusal and resistance; and the survivor's capacity to bear inhuman hardship, his small victories against the monolith of destruction, are the forms of life-inspired stubbornness. From this point of view the survivor's struggle is largely negative. It may have a positive outcome; by living through a situation he may alter it, but this end the survivor will not count on. And there are situations, like those of Solzhenitsyn's heroes, entirely beyond the individual's influence. But this circumstance need not set a limit to the survivor's significance. . . .

The survivor does not choose his fate; extremity descends upon him as upon millions of people in the twentieth century. He would escape it if he could, but finds himself in a place of imploding evil that from every side drives him toward death. Solzhenitsyn takes us to the heart of this experience, and it is in his work that the heroism of survival is most earnestly celebrated.

Solzhenitsyn's survivor is the man ardently in love with his people and their cause; the man who stood against the Nazi onslaught only to find himself thrown into a Siberian labour camp. This same man, helpless but fiercely unreconciled to victimhood, is determined to remain a human being, innocent and unbroken, under conditions specifically devised to crush out life and spirit. His energies burn with the pointed fury of an extreme tension between the will to live and the will to remain pure—between an almost mystical appreciation of life, on the one hand, and on the other an unwavering refusal to capitulate, sell out, or in any way become accessory to a system which reduces men to puppets and meat.

This is the survivor's predicament, and from it, with the intimate authority of one who has fully suffered his subject, Solzhenitsyn draws an image of man for whom the struggle to keep a living soul in a living body becomes the *sine qua non* of moral being—and in this stark sense the definitively human act. . . .

MOVE BEYOND DESPAIR

Shukhov, the simple-hearted hero of *One Day in the Life of Ivan Denisovich* is this kind of man. He has been unjustly imprisoned, and has lived years of days of sub-zero weather without decent clothing or a warm place to sleep, rising each day before the sun to twelve hours of heavy labour on a starvation diet. He steers his life through sickness and exhaustion, through the random cruelty of camp procedure and the betrayal of fellow prisoners ready to sell their souls or another's life for a few ounces of bread. And yet he is not broken: "even eight years as a convict hadn't turned him into a jackal—and the longer he spent at the camp the stronger he made himself."

Shukhov is willing to give way to other *zeks* [prisoners], to perform services for men he respects, but will not make a deal with power or authority, never inform, never do a favour for the cooks or ask one of them. He has developed the *zek*'s special ability to cheat the officials and camp regulations, by which he saves his strength and now and then gets an extra bowl of soup (these are major victories), but he will not cheat others in the same situation as himself. And through it all he maintains an elementary sense of self-respect:

> Every nerve in his body was taut, all his longing was concentrated in that cigarette butt—which meant more to him now, it seemed, than freedom itself—but he would never lower himself like that Fetiukov, he would never look at a man's mouth.

Due to his situation as much as to his character, Shukhov has come a long way in the wisdom of simplicity. He has learned to extract immense satisfaction—a sense of animal well-being which saves him from self-pity and despair— from slight and infrequent moments of pleasure. Working with his squad to build a wall (the temperature is -17°), Shukhov is inspired to delight by the rhythm of the work and the interplay of skills; he enjoys the warmth which spreads through his body, and later, the deeper joy of a job well done. He has, in short, learned to fully appreciate every inch of life that transcends pain and hopelessness.

In this respect, by far the most important event in his life is food, and like all of Solzhenitsyn's heroes, Shukhov has developed an extraordinary attitude toward the watered-down soup and black bread which sustain him. To eat becomes a ritualised experience in which the resurrection of bodily joy—or rather, since he never gets enough, the heightened tension of desire on the verge of fulfilment—becomes the physical ground of faith in the value of life. Souptime becomes a "sacred moment," a revelation deep in the body's pleasure that, at bottom and in spite of everything, life is strong and worth its pain:

> Shukhov took off his hat and laid it on his knee. He tasted one bowl, he tasted the other. Not bad—there was some fish in it . . .

> He dug in. First he only drank the broth, drank and drank. As it went down, filling his whole body with warmth, all of his guts began to flutter inside him at their meeting with that stew. Goo-ood!

> And now Shukov complained about nothing: neither about the length of his stretch, nor about the length of the day, nor about their swiping another Sunday. This was all he thought about now: we'll survive. We'll stick it out. God willing, till it's over.

Extremity intensifies experience, purifies it, forces men to the essence of their encounters with reality. Only sex (and how like sexual climax Shukhov's ritual is) comes close in that it too may issue in the physical intuition of a goodness at life's core. Shukhov eats his soup, and bliss wells up like a visitation, like an extravagant blessing, as though this second bowl, tricked from the cooks, were the fullest beneficence of God. Like some of Tolstoy's characters—Pierre, Levin—Shukhov attains that rarest of moments, when a man is simply, and against all evidence, happy to be alive.

ON THE EDGE OF HAPPINESS

What Solzhenitsyn means is clear: *You have not beaten us down.* The whole point of *Ivan Denisovich* is that yes, such a man exists in such a place. If we miss this we miss everything the survivor is about. Surrounded by the combined inhumanity of man and nature, this small simple man has made a life for himself, with its grossly handicapped balance of pain and pleasure, risk and victory, deprivation and fulfilment. And to a slight but all-important degree, it is *his* life; each act in violation of camp regulations, each moment of pleasure, lifts him anew above the sheer necessity which the agents of dehumanisation thought to impose upon him.

We may find it difficult to comprehend, but Solzhenitsyn's hero lives on the edge of happiness. Of course Shukhov suffers; we cannot forget that *this* day was uncommon for luck, and that pain is the substantial element in which he lives, as present and cruelly persistent as the Siberian winter. But he has come to terms with it, transcended his situation by refusing self-pity or despair or the temptation to hope for anything but life itself, and then gone on to find what goodness he can in the life he has.

Shukhov and His Peasant Virtues

Christopher Moody

Solzhenitsyn has chosen Ivan Denisovich Shukhov as the central character of his novel in order to highlight a simple peasant's responses to human suffering. Author Christopher Moody points out that Shukhov's characteristics—compassion, self-respect, sturdiness, and practical wisdom—are native to the Russian peasant. He adds that it is these homegrown talents that eventually allow Shukhov to survive the harshness of life in the concentration camp.

By choosing peasants as the central protagonists of *One Day in the Life of Ivan Denisovich,* Solzhenitsyn was upholding one of the enduring traditions of Russian literature. For the aristocrats of the nineteenth century, the peasant held an almost mystical fascination. He was idealised by Leo Tolstoy, Ivan Turgenev and Viktor Nekrasov in their search for truth, as the repository of natural wisdom and simplicity. It was this wishful image which Anton Chekhov and Ivan Bunin attempted to correct with their ruthlessly objective glimpses of peasant life at the end of the century. Soviet critics were quick to see both these views reflected in Solzhenitsyn's novel. "Reading the story," wrote one about *One Day,* "I involuntarily compared it with Tolstoy's folk tales, with their admiration of passive saintliness and the meekness of the 'simple folk'. Solzhenitsyn even selected his hero on the principle that holy simplicity is higher than any wisdom." Another, however, complained that Shukhov's way of life was little better than that of an animal, "a total egoist, living only for his belly.". . .

There is a superficial resemblance between Shukhov and Tolstoy's Platon Karataev, skilfully sewing a shirt for the French corporal. Karataev "knew how to do everything, he was always busy," while Shukhov "knew how to manage everything." But the parallel between the two is confined to their external characteristics. In Shukhov there is nothing of "the unfathomable, rounded, eternal personification of the spirit of simplicity and truth" which Pierre thought he had found in Karataev. Nor is Shukhov in any meaningful sense a religious believer. Solzhenitsyn does not idealise Shukhov or hold him up as the embodiment of some abstract principle. It happens to be Shukhov's nature that he is simple and submissive. Such qualities were cultivated as the essential prerequisites for survival even by more assertive characters like Tiurin. It is the lesson of the camps which Buinovsky must learn. And Shukhov's practical wisdom and adroitness are no more than refinements in a man accustomed to earn his living by the use of his hands.

During the early discussions between the "friends and foes of Ivan Denisovich" opinions were divided as to whether Shukhov had managed to retain his pride and personal integrity or whether "in reconciling himself to the camps he (had) surrendered his human traits entirely to his basic instincts." One critic concluded that "the regime of the special camps destroyed the souls of all the inmates and left them only a single goal—to stay alive by any means at all." It was true that as Vladimir Lakshin described it,

> the entire system of imprisonment in the camps through which Ivan Denisovich passed was calculated to suppress mercilessly, to kill all feelings of right and legality in man, to demonstrate in matters large and small an impunity for arbitrariness against which any outburst of noble indignation was powerless. The camp administration did not allow the convicts to forget even for a moment that they were deprived of rights, and that arbitrariness was the only judge.

In such a situation, there must have been many who gave in and succumbed to the degradation inflicted upon them. This is not true of Shukhov and his fellow prisoners who, with the exception perhaps of the informers and Fetiukov, are shown not only adapting well enough to survive, but also maintaining their self respect. But for prisoners who had been in so long that they had forgotten their past and with so little hope of release that they could conceive of no future, it was inevitable that they should lose the habit of planning ahead: "scrape through today and hope for tomorrow." All the happenings which make Shukhov's day "almost a happy one" refer to that day alone. Tomorrow he must begin all over again.

The moments Shukhov lives for, on which he focuses his whole being, are the meagre sensual pleasures a prisoner can enjoy. Meals, those sacred moments for which a *zek* [prisoner] lives, are eaten with slow concentration, "you had to eat with your whole mind on your food." When he manages to scrounge a cigarette "the smoke crept and flowed through his whole hungry body, making his head and feet respond to it." Keeping warm is a primary concern of all the prisoners but the horizons of many no doubt extend beyond Shukhov's preoccupation with food. . . .

TIMID BUT NOT SERVILE

By nature a timid man, it is easier for Shukhov "who knew of no way of standing up for his rights" to learn the necessary degree of servility, than for some others: "better to growl and submit, if you were stubborn they broke you." The Captain, the only one who tries to hit back at his persecutors, has only been in camp a few weeks. But he too will learn to survive by emulating the other *zeks,* "inert but wary."

Shukhov is ready to run errands for his fellow prisoners and perform services which will bring him some small advantage, but not at the sacrifice of his own sense of personal worth. "He wouldn't take on any old job." He keeps himself tidy and clean. He is prepared to scrounge a smoke but "he would never lower himself like that Fetiukov, he would never look at another man's mouth." He retains his dignity, "he couldn't eat with his hat on", and certain little personal fads such as, for instance, not eating fish eyes.

On several occasions throughout his "happy day" Shukhov exhibits a compassion and humanity which a murderously inhumane environment has not crushed out of him. In spite of his longing to receive a parcel, he has self-lessly forbidden his wife to send one so that his children may be better fed. He feels genuine sorrow for the Captain, and for Tsezar when he risks having his parcel stolen. He shares his cigarettes with the deaf Senka and his biscuits with Alesha, two characters who are even less equipped than he to stand up for themselves. Shukhov's integrity and ingrained sense of right and wrong have also survived in camp. He deplores the idea of saving his own skin at the expense of someone else's blood, like the squealers. And he'd never take a bribe, "even eight years as a convict hadn't turned him into a jackal." On the contrary, he has even acquired an inner strength, "the longer he stayed in the camp, the stronger he made himself."

The portrait which emerges of Ivan Shukhov, is of an unexceptional little man, wielding the practical guile native to the Russian peasant, simple but not innocent, sly but not dishonest, insulted but not a weakling, and submissive but not degraded. A man with sufficient force of character not only to preserve his primitive moral sense and feelings of common decency but even to benefit in some small way from his ordeal. Shukhov commands pity but also respect. Those who complained that his behaviour in camp was unworthy of a Soviet man were doing him less than justice. But if they meant that none of the qualities exhibited by Shukhov and the other prisoners were particularly attributable to their Soviet or socialist upbringing they were right. A year after *One Day,* at the height of the controversy it generated, a short novel entitled *They Endured,* by Boris Dyakov, was published. It was an undisguised polemic against *One Day.* "The figures of the communists are central in the story," wrote a sympathetic critic, "unbending faith in communist ideals, in the durability of Soviet power, in the triumph of justice, and a warm love for the homeland—that is what enabled them not only to survive physically, but to preserve their ideological staunchness and their human qualities." In *One Day,* there is no suggestion that the virtues which enabled the prisoners to endure came from anywhere but their own inner being. As in *The First Circle* and *Cancer Ward* each prisoner is ultimately thrown back on his own personal resources. Rubin and Rusanov, the communists in the big novels, do not cope better than the rest. In *One Day,* the only character to invoke the name of communism is the Captain, a camp novice. And he must learn to sublimate his ideals, not parade them. If there is a doctrine which fortifies the prisoners in the camp, it is the camp itself. It is the camp which has toughened Shukhov just as it made Kostoglotov in *Cancer Ward* "sharp as an axe." The hardy Tiurin is also "a true son of Gulag." It was this lack of clear ideological orientation which finally disqualified *One Day* from official favor when a more orthodox interpretation of socialist realism began to be applied after Khrushchev's departure.

Solzhenitsyn has observed that "Russian literature has always been sensitive to human suffering." In a sense all his own works are studies in human suffering and of differing responses to it. Shukhov's submissiveness is partly a cultivated quality, but in other ways he is a positive character who actively resists suffering by the exercise of certain sturdy, down-to-earth virtues. . . .

WORK ETHIC

Soviet defenders of Ivan Denisovich and Matryona were able to quote one feature of the characters' personalities which coincides entirely with the requirements of socialist ideology, namely their attitude to work. The work ethic in Soviet literature has been much emphasised, but that it was also a nineteenth-century tradition may be seen in such writers as Chekhov and Tolstoy. . . .

Solzhenitsyn does not idealise creative labour in *One Day*. Only Shukhov among the prisoners adopts a genuinely conscientious attitude to work. When reading of the idleness prevailing in his native village, he reflects that "easy money weighs light in the hand and doesn't give you the feeling you've earned it. There was truth in the old saw: pay short money and you get short value. He still had a good pair of hands, capable hands. Surely, when he was out, he'd find work as a stone-setter or carpenter, or tinker?" Solzhenitsyn makes a further discrimination between constructive work and pointless, humiliating work. When he is ordered to mop out the guardroom, Shukhov does as shoddy a job as he can get away with. When doing something meaningful, however, as on the building site, he is ready to make an effort and enjoys his work. But of all his team only he can muster real enthusiasm and pride in what he is doing. For Shukhov alone does work offer a liberation. Before the war he had been a builder and so the opportunity to exercise his skill even under the machine-guns of the guards is an act of freedom. It increases his sense of personal worth: "after working like that he felt equal to the team leaders." For most of the others, especially the intellectuals, physical labour was the most burdensome part of their bondage. And even for Shukhov his enthusiasm is the euphoria of the moment. In camp he thinks to himself of the doctor who recommended work as the antidote for illness: "you can overwork a horse to death. The doctor ought to understand. If he'd been sweating blood laying blocks he'd quieten down, you could be sure of that.". . .

One Day provides a picture of goodness and truth at the mercy of evil and falsehood. The innocent are inexorably crushed by the evil of the camp regime, to which the icy grip of winter adds symbolic reinforcement. The story becomes a parable of everyday life in Russia. And it is also, as Max Hayward has suggested,

> a moving statement of universal application about the human lot . . . It is symbolic of human existence as is Kafka's *Trial.* The day in the life of Ivan Denisovich is a day in *anybody's* life. The majority of the human race are trapped in a monotonous daily routine which differs from the concentration camp only in the *degree* of its unpleasantness and hopelessness.

CHAPTER 3

One Day: Form and Style

READINGS ON
ONE DAY IN THE LIFE OF
IVAN DENISOVICH

Narrative Style and Plot Structure

Richard Luplow

Richard Luplow, literary critic and scholar, says that it is not enough to view *One Day* as a political novel; it should be read as a narrative. Solzhenitsyn's themes of survival and human dignity are dependent on the author's skillful narrative style. Luplow further maintains that much of the work's authenticity derives from Solzhenitsyn's carefully wrought use of point of view, voice, contrast, plot structure, understatement, and irony. He discusses two of the novel's strategies: *skaz*, a kind of narrative that uses the speech habits and point of view of a fictional narrator who usually has a lowly background, and quasi-direct discourse, which blends the author's comments with those of the hero.

It is my contention that in general no one particular aspect of a literary work should be discussed in the context of that work alone without relating this aspect to . . . the work's basic unifying theme. Therefore, before going into the discussion of narrative style and plot structure, I shall begin by defining the basic theme of *One Day in the Life of Ivan Denisovich*. It is an affirmation of man's will for survival and his capability of achieving and maintaining dignity under almost unbelievably inhuman conditions which work against the possibility of survival. The theme is, in a sense, "existential"—in that it strongly affirms a simple man's persistent will to survive by making the best of and living for the present moment, regardless of the difficult circumstances, their inhumanity and absurdity. . . . This theme combines a striving both for survival and for dignity. . . .

Given this . . . underlying theme of *One Day,* an analysis of how . . . this theme is realized, should be focused on . . .

Excerpted from Richard Luplow, "Narrative Style and Structure in *One Day in the Life of Ivan Denisovich," Russian Literature Triquarterly,* Fall 1971. Reprinted by permission of Ardis Publishers.

the plot structure and the narrative system. The plot is organized into a structure of contrasts which brings to life, makes significant, and infuses with a pathetic sense of joy the above-mentioned existential moments—while the narrative system, though rather complex, is based primarily on the realization of a sense of unity, a feeling for the wholeness and the authenticity of the experience being described.

To define the narrative system one must use two important concepts . . . : quasi-direct discourse *(nesobstvenno-primaia rech')* and *skaz.*

REPRESENTED DISCOURSE AND *SKAZ*

Quasi-direct discourse is a type of represented (i.e. not quoted) discourse which has distinct characteristics of the spoken language of a given character, although the character is referred to in the third person—specifically, vocabulary, idioms, and syntax on a slang, substandard, folkish, highly emotional, or purely conversational level, and the absence of strictly literary forms of expression. Such discourse is not linked to the character-referent by direct grammatical connectives, such as "He was thinking that . . ." or "He had the feeling then that . . ." and so on. The link between quasi-direct discourse and the character-referent is made, rather, simply by sentence contiguity or implication. . . .

Third-person *skaz* can be defined as a consistent use of the general speech characteristics of quasi-direct discourse with a third-person implicit narrator as referent. Such third-person *skaz* narration does not necessarily proceed as if the narrator were directly speaking to the reader, but may instead, as here, take the form of a written narration which is oriented toward or individualized by speech patterns characteristic of the environment being depicted in the work. Within this latter form, then, there may appear strictly literary or non-spoken grammatical forms of expression. . . .

TWO DISTINCT VOICES

There are two distinct narrative voices in *One Day:* the voice of a *skaz* narrator, which is the controlling voice of the novel, and the voice of Ivan Denisovich Shukhov, represented through quasi-direct discourse. For the most part the *skaz* narration proceeds as if there were a narrator speaking in his own voice, but looking at the action over Shukhov's shoulder as it were, seeing only what he would see. Also, a good deal of the action is presented directly through Shukhov's consciousness, that is, in Shukhov's own voice, portrayed by means of quasi-direct discourse. These two voices together thus focus maximum attention on the character and experiences of Shukhov. . . .

Very often these two voices (narrative *skaz* and Shukhov) blend together to such an extent that in many passages they cannot be told apart with certainty. Thus, the *skaz* narrator's voice comes to represent the generalized voice of the prisoners in such a way that it includes Shukhov's voice as the dominant one within the general blending or mixture. This blending of voices gives a strong sense of the unity or wholeness of the camp experience being portrayed.

There is, at the same time, an important contrastive feature within this narrative system. The main narrative voice, and to a certain extent the blended voices, focuses the reader's attention on the whole camp environment around Shukhov, while the distinct Shukhov voice places the reader directly in his consciousness and gives us his experiences as they relate to this environment. And finally, the fact that these two voices do resemble each other as distinct entities at the same time as they often merge and blend gives a feeling of authenticity or convincingness to the entire narration.

The following are characteristic examples of these different narrative voices. First, Shukhov's voice as portrayed in quasi-direct discourse:

> But this moment was ours! While the authorities worked things out, you could squeeze in somewhere where it was a little warmer and sit down and rest for a while—there'd be plenty of time yet to break your back. It was good if you could got near a stove, you could undo your foot-cloths and warm 'em up some. Then your feet would be warm all day long. But even without a stove it was still great.

Next, the narrator's voice:

> . . . Nearby them at the table sat Captain Buinovsky. He had long ago finished his mush, and he didn't know that the gang had extra ones, and he didn't look around to see how many of them his gang boss still had left. He simply relaxed and warmed himself up. He didn't have the strength to get up and go out into the freezing weather, or into the cold warm-up room which didn't warm up anybody anyway. Right now he was occupying a place he had no right to and hindering the newly arrived gangs, just like those who five minutes ago he had chased out with his metallic voice. He was new in camp, only recently on the work squad. It was moments like this (al-

though he didn't know it) that were especially important for him, moments which were transforming him from an imperious, loudmouth naval officer into a slow-moving and circumspect camp prisoner. And only his being changed this way was making him able to get through the twenty five years of imprisonment which now loomed before him.

And finally, a passage in which the narrator's and Shukhov's voices are blended together.

> The outer door creaked as Shukhov opened it, and then an inner one, padded with rope, creaked too. Letting in a cloud of icy cold air, he went inside and quickly pulled the door shut (hurrying so they wouldn't yell at him, "Hey, you bastard, shut the door!").

> It seemed real hot to him in the office, just like a steam bath. The sun coming in through the melting ice on the window-panes was playing happily—not angry like on top of the power plant. And big puffs of smoke from Caesar's pipe were spreading through the sunbeam like incense in a church. The bastards had gotten the stove going so hot it glowed red right through. Even the flues were red-hot.

> Just sit down for a minute in heat like that and you'd fall asleep on the spot.

> The office had two rooms. The door of the second one, the work supervisor's, wasn't quite closed, and through it his voice was thundering . . .

SHUKHOV'S DISTINCT VOICE

The following then are the more salient characteristics of the distinct Shukhov voice. First, Shukhov's voice is marked by conversationally (and very frequently emotionally tinged) clipped, broken, or incomplete sentences, such as *"Glazom po otvesu. Glazom plashmia. Skhvacheno. Sleduiushchii!"* [A look perpendicular. A look flatwise. Got it. Next one!] Second, Shukhov's voice uses colloquialisms and very folksy elements, especially folk-type sayings which are often in symmetrical parallel syntax form, and are often rhymed. For example: *"Kto kogo smozhet, tot togo i glozhet"* [Fig: Everyone for himself]; *". . . ne vykusish'—ne vyprosish'"* [Fig: If you don't grab for a thing you won't get it]. Third, Shukhov's voice frequently uses the second person singular as an example or illustration of something, almost as if Shukhov were talking directly to the reader, as in:

> . . . You had to eat with all your thoughts on the food—like now, you see, you bite off these small pieces of bread, and you

work them around with your tongue, and you suck them into
your cheeks—and that way it tasted so good, that soggy black
bread.

Fourth, it uses typically oral grammatical forms. Especially
frequent is the use of second person singular imperatives in
uniquely conversational, emotional ways. For example, a brief
description of the mess hall in the morning in Shukhov's voice
ends with the one-word sentence: *"Zakhodi!"* (Enter). It is
used in the sense of *"Mozhno bylo priamo zakhodit'"* (You
could go right in). Or there is the use of *"Zhdi"* (Wait) in the
sense of *"Nado bylo by zhdat'"* (You'd have to wait). Finally,
there is the use of the first person *plural* grammatical forms,
most frequently the possessive pronoun *"nash"* (our) and the
first person plural subjectless verbs, but also on a few occasions the actual pronoun *"my"* (we). This characteristic, which
is also, but less frequently, found in nondistinct or blended
voice passages, is a striking distortion of the usual quasi-direct
discourse form as described above. The next example is from
the scene in which Shukhov's work gang is racing another one
back to the camp at night:

> Our column had reached the street now, while the one from
> the tool works had passed out of sight behind a housing
> block. The race went on blindly.

> Our column had it easier here, down the middle of the street.
> And our guards, too, had less to stumble over at the sides.
> This was where we had to gain ground on them.

The distinctive voice of the *skaz* narrator has both oral
and written characteristics. It does have in common with
Shukhov's speech the frequent use of the camp prisoners'
particular lexicon, their slang and non-standard vocabulary,
and it occasionally expresses opinions regarding the camp
situation as if from the prisoners' point of view. In general,
however, it features a more literary style, characterized by:
relatively complete, straightforward, grammatically correct
sentences; the absence of direct emotional statements in
conversational syntax; and the use of more literary grammatical forms, such as active participles. This voice has already been adequately illustrated above.

Besides these narrative voices, there is a great deal of direct discourse which has many characteristics in common
with the narrative voices described above.

It should be noted, finally, that although for the most part
the narrator's voice stands for the generalized voice of the

camp prisoners, expressed in a fairly literary style, occasionally this voice is localized or specified in a given scene to a given group of prisoners, or briefly to one specific prisoner, using Shukhov-like quasi-direct discourse with them as referent. An example of this technique is the scene in which members of Shukhov's impatient work gang are greeting the missing prisoner who has held them up at the end of the day. This is part of the overall blending of different narrative voices through the use of similar or identical characteristics within each of them, with a resulting unified and convincing effect.

A Separate View

The narrative system, in addition to creating a sense of unity and convincingness regarding the camp experiences, and providing the contrastive function within the narrative already described, has some other specific functions which will now be analyzed.

There are, first of all, certain functions of the narrator's voice which are made possible by the presence of a narrator's point of view separate from Shukhov's. One of these functions is the fairly frequent use of literary, condensed, and complete descriptions of certain scenes. Shukhov himself would not realistically notice with such completeness or with so compact a style these scenes or particular aspects of them. Another function of the narrator's separate voice is to occasionally give information which Shukhov would not have access to. For example, he describes what the "medic" in the infirmary is doing as Shukhov waits, as Shukhov can't see him. And occasionally he goes briefly into a character's mind to describe his thoughts.

But by far the most important function of the separate narrator point of view is what I would call a "making objective" function regarding Shukhov. (This is similar to the *ostranenie* or "making strange" function of shifting points of view found in [Leo] Tolstoy.) As noted above, the main focus is on Shukhov's character as he reacts to his surroundings, and the *skaz* elements in the narrator's voice tend to blend or unify his and Shukhov's voices closely together to create one whole experience. However, the presence of a narrator's voice distinct from Shukhov's makes it possible for him, and therefore for the reader, to step out of Shukhov's subjective consciousness and view him more objectively in some scenes. This gives a more rounded view. One example is the scene at the work site in which Shukhov is waiting for a possible handout from Caesar, but is ignored.

> "Hm, hm!" Shukhov cleared his throat. He didn't have the nerve to interrupt this learned conversation. But then there wasn't any sense in just standing there either.

> Caesar turned around and stuck out his hand for the mush, not even looking at Shukhov, as though the mush had come to him by itself out of thin air . . .

> Shukhov stood there just as long as was decent for a man who had brought a bowl of mush. He was waiting to see if Caesar might offer him a smoke. But Caesar had quite forgotten him, that Shukhov was standing right here behind him.

> So Shukhov turned around and quietly went out.

Shukhov's separate voice in quasi-direct discourse also has specific functions. First, it is the chief means of characterizing Shukhov. There is an almost complete absence of physical description of him. We learn about him almost entirely through the particular presentation of his voice, through what he has to say. Secondly, this technique creates a sense of immediacy, since we are in Shukhov's consciousness experiencing things as he does and reacting to them with him. This latter function is accompanied by that strange combination, vis-a-vis the reader, of simultaneous involvement and detachment which quasi-direct discourse gives.

As already noted, the plot is structured on a series of contrasts which bring to life for Shukhov the meaningful moments of his day. This contrastive structure operates on two levels, and on each level a consistent type of verbal irony is used. On one level there is the presentation of the camp environment, the horrible conditions in which the men have to live as best they can, and the circumstances of their absurd incarceration and endless sentences. On this level the irony of matter-of-fact understatement is used. For example, grim facts about the prisoners' present lives and the reasons for their imprisonment are matter-of-factly, almost casually mentioned. . . .

IRONY THROUGH UNDERSTATEMENT

The story of Shukhov's own "treason" during the war is another example. In 1942 he was captured by the Germans, and after escaping he made the mistake of returning to his

own people, where he was automatically arrested for treason and given the choice of being shot or signing a confes-
sion of guilt.

> The way Shukhov had it figured, it was very simple. If he didn't
> sign he'd be six feet under; if he did sign, he'd go on living at least
> a while longer. He signed.

The final example of this irony of understatement is the last
paragraph of the book, explaining that the three added days
are due to leap years.

The irony here is basically a matter of [the reader's] point
of view and the narrator's toward Shukhov and his situation,
and not a matter of Shukhov's point of view. This is another
aspect of the "making objective" function of the narrator's
voice. Shukhov himself constantly rationalizes his situation.
While talking to himself in one scene he imagines how
things will be at home when he finally gets there, and imagines himself actually being there. But later he argues to himself that he is clearly better off where he is now, that they
wouldn't let him go home anyway, and that there's no telling
what would happen if they did let him out.

This irony of understatement on the camp environment
level is not all-encompassing. There are also strong positive
statements of bitterness, hatred, and disgust, but they are directed almost exclusively toward individuals in the camp's
ruling hierarchy, and not towards the camp (or state) system
itself.

A STUDY OF CONTRASTS

Contrasted to this presentation of the camp situation is a
whole series of what I would call Shukhov's "small successes," that is, positive accomplishments which are in-
significant in our terms, from our point of view, but which
from Shukhov's point of view, and in contrast to his environment, become real successes. They are expressed very
emotionally in Shukhov's own voice; they give him a great
deal of happiness, pride, and dignity, and are, in fact, precisely what give him the will to survive. . . .

Some of the most striking examples of these successes, the
ones with the greatest psychological effect on Shukhov, are:
his work gang beating the other one back to camp; Shukhov
getting a small bit of steel past the search and his feeling of
"walking on air" afterwards; his comment on the joys of
sleeping after breakfast on Sunday; the sense of "freedom" felt

in the evening, especially the freedom to talk and express opinions; the long awaited bowl of watery-thin gruel with just a bit of fish in it—which he eats with such real satisfaction, so that nothing in his situation bothers him any longer.

CONTRARY VIEW

Norman Podhoretz, editor of Commentary, *finds it difficult to identify with the very difficult life of the main character.*

Tvardovsky . . . pronounced *Ivan Denisovich* superior to Dostoevsky's *House of the Dead* because "there we see the people through the eyes of an intellectual, whereas here the intellectuals are seen through the eyes of the people." On this issue, however, even many admirers of *Ivan Denisovich* disagreed, asking why Solzhenitsyn had chosen to write from the point of view of a simple peasant instead of through the consciousness of an intellectual. Solzhenitsyn hotly defended himself against this criticism:

> Of course, it would have been simpler and easier to write about an intellectual (doubtless thinking of oneself all the while: "What a fine fellow I am and how I suffered"). But . . . having been flung together with [Ivan Denisovich] Shukhov in the same sort of conditions, . . . a complete nobody as far as the others were concerned and indistinguishable from the rest of them, . . . I had a chance to feel exactly the same as they.

[Michael] Scammell, agreeing with Tvardovsky and Solzhenitsyn against the critics, adds that "By making his hero a common peasant, Solzhenitsyn was able to seize the essence of the labor-camp experience and universalize it. An intellectual hero would have been less typical and more particular, diluting the story's power and impact."

Surely, however, the impact of the story is weakened, not strengthened, by being told through a character whose life on the outside has been as full of hardship and deprivation as Ivan Denisovich Shukhov's and who has therefore become so accustomed to the kind of conditions he is forced to endure in the labor camp that he can end a day of unrelieved horror in a state of happiness over all the luck he has had in not suffering even more ("They hadn't put him in the cooler. The gang hadn't been chased out to work in the Socialist Community Development. . . . They hadn't found that piece of steel in the frisk," etc.). Solzhenitsyn intended this conclusion as a celebration of the resiliency of the human spirit, and so it is. But at the same time it makes identifying with Ivan Denisovich Shukhov (or entering into his skin, to use Solzhenitsyn's image) almost insuperably difficult.

Norman Podhoretz, "The Terrible Question of Aleksandr Solzhenitsyn," *Commentary*, February 1985.

The presentation of these small successes culminates when he recounts some of the best of them to himself just before going to sleep at night, "entirely pleased" now at the end of such a good day. . . .

Statements to the effect that *One Day* lacks a plot are, it seems to me, not to the point at all. The gradual build-up of this second level of the structure, reaching one apex in the middle of the novel and culminating as quoted above, versus the general elaboration of details on the first level *is* the plot.

At one point, during the noon break, Shukhov happens to overhear, but significantly, does not understand, a brief discussion of [Sergey] Eisenstein's film *Ivan the Terrible,* in which Caesar argues that it is basically not the what of the film that matters, but the how. He defends Eisenstein for distorting the particular historical content (necessary because of censorship) for the sake of its successful esthetic form. . . . There is a deeper level of thematic irony here, in the sense that the novel sets up an ironic contrast between the "official" significance of the work for the State, i.e. its continuance and development in order to keep the present prisoners and to imprison more of them, and the "real" significance of this work for the individual prisoner. Among Shukhov's small successes, work is the ultimate success for him, and he recognizes it as a source of real dignity and pride for himself. The center of the novel is concerned with this work, and it plays a large role in the theme. . . . The extent to which he becomes absorbed in his work is strongly stressed. Near the end of the long work day he even expends a few precious minutes of voluntary overtime in order to finish a section of his job properly. Part of the indication of this total absorption is the fact that the description of Shukhov's work in building the wall is done, in great detail, in Shukhov's own voice, while most other descriptions of the camp are given in the narrator's voice, since realistically these things would no longer be noticed by Shukhov. This is another example of how carefully Solzhenitsyn manipulates point of view. This relation of Shukhov to his work is thus part of the basic structure of contrasts between the camp environment and Shukhov's reaction to it, what he makes of it.

Another important aspect of the structure of contrasts is the presentation of other characters who contrast with Shukhov in how they react to and try to survive in the camp. There are those, first of all, who are higher in the camp hi-

erarchy and who survive comfortably through regular re-
ceipt of valuable packages from "outside," packages which
allow them to bribe their way into soft jobs and eat better.
Caesar is the main example. The point of contrast lies in the
fact that such prisoners are shown to survive well, but to
lack any dignity in doing so, since they survive not by their
own means or the kind of dignity that Shukhov achieves
through his work. Then there are the "scavengers" (a constant epithet) such as Fetyukov, who try to survive through
base means. . . .

The point, then, is clear. Survival itself, in some cases, and
meaningful or "respectable" survival in others, depends on
the prisoner's ability to find a way of achieving and maintaining a sense of dignity and self-respect within the circumstances of the camp. We have seen that for Shukhov
work is the primary source of this dignity. There are many
other examples of how Shukhov, and other prisoners who
are dignified in Shukhov's eyes, maintain this sense of dignity in their actions. . . .

In summary, then, it is primarily through the complex
manipulation of narrative style and point of view that *One
Day* achieves its thematic complexity and unity and creates
a sense of the authenticity and immediacy of the camp experience. And it is through this narrative system that the
complex set of thematic and structural contrasts is organized and is underscored by the use of levels of irony.

Popular Speech: Toward Simplicity and Significance

Leonid Rzhevsky

Author Leonid Rzhevsky maintains that Solzhenitsyn's artistic achievement is in revealing the life of
Ivan Denisovich "from within." Solzhenitsyn
achieves this through the narrator and the language
he uses: common speech, slang, and prison jargon.
The language traits of an educated narrator merge
with those of a semi-literate worker, causing the
reader to identify the storyteller with Shukhov himself. Rzhevsky, a literary scholar, has taught Slavic
literature at the University of Oklahoma, Norwich
University, and New York University

"It is hard to imagine that only in 1963 we did not know the
name Solzhenitsyn. It seems that he has been alive in our literature for a long time, and without him it would decidedly
be incomplete."

The quotation is taken from Vladimir Lakshin's article
"Ivan Denisovich—His Friends and Enemies," the best
among the numerous critical responses to this work, at least
in the Russian language.

In his analysis Lakshin managed to find and to name the
crux of the author's art, that which helped Solzhenitsyn's
narrative become a literary event. "Solzhenitsyn," said Lakshin, "writes so that we see and learn about the life of a convict not from the sidelines but from within, 'from him.'"

This "from within" is splendid! It is a pity that polemical
themes diverted the author of the article from an investigation of this "from within." It must be pursued. . . .

In *One Day in the Life of Ivan Denisovich*, . . . someone
takes the reader firmly by the hand, leads him behind the

From *Solzhenitsyn: Creator and Heroic Deed*, by Leonid Rzhevsky, translated by Sonja
Miller (Tuscaloosa: University of Alabama Press, 1978). Copyright © 1978 Leonid
Rzhevsky.

barbed wire and into a day of prison life. And, without releasing the reader's hand, he comments upon this day in a confidential manner that charms the reader. For in this manner there is neither fear nor insecurity, nor twaddle.

This is exposing "from within."

To understand the nature of this means to clarify the image of this "someone"—the narrator, with whose eyes the reader watches the events of the day—the *zeks* [prisoners], the friskings, the conflicts, the squads. This image is revealed first of all in the language of the work.

The presence of the narrator and the spoken quality of the narrative constitute the features of *skaz* [a traditional narrative based on folk speech and colored by the personality of the narrator]. In Solzhenitsyn's narrative the spoken style is interspersed with information in a formal literary style. It is of course the author himself who sits at a desk and describes, for example, the naval captain Buinovsky. "A guilty smile parted the chapped lips of the captain who had sailed around Europe and the Great Northern Route. And he bent down, happy over the half scoop of thin oatmeal—no grease, just oats and water."

Also, many of the novel's dialogues are given not in the spoken style common for *skaz*, but with precise verbal characteristics peculiar to the speaker. For example, Tzesar and Buinovsky argue about the film *The Battleship Potemkin*.

"Yes. . . . But navy life is a little bit doll-like there."

"You see, we have been spoiled by modern screen techniques. . . ."

However, the principal element that prevails in the narrative is oral speech—the language of *skaz*, the roots of which are found in an oral *počvennost'* in daily, historical, and dialect layers of folk speech—primarily in ordinary conversation.

The words are from common speech. Here the common speech belongs to a particular locale; it includes prison camp jargon: *oper* ("operations worker"), *popki* ("guards in the watchtowers"), *polkany* ("workers in the messhall"), *pridurki* ("those who manage to get themselves easy assignments"), *šmon* ("search or frisk").

Here is some more generally used slang: *zagnut'* ("to say the improbable"), *vkalyvat'* ("to work zealously"), *maternut'* ("to curse"), *gvozdanut'* ("to nail", in the sense of hit), *nedotyka* ("a dope"), *žituxa* (from *žizn'*—"life"), etc. Here are Solzhenitsyn's "restorations" for the literary language from

Dahl's dictionary: *ežeden* ("everyday"), zakalelyj ("frozen"), *ljut'* ("fierceness"), etc. Finally, the language overheard or created by the author himself in the spirit of common usage, such as: *prigrebat'sja* ("to find fault with"), *podsosat'sja* ("to get a place")—"*Tut že i Fetjukov, šakal, podsosalsja*" (Immediately then Fetiukov, the jackal, found a place); *razmorčivyj* ("relaxed"), etc.

Colloquial prison camp speech is plentiful: *kačat' prava* ("to demand what is laid down by the law"), *xodit' stučat k kumu* ("to denounce"). There are many proverbial expressions, composing three different groups: *(a)* borrowings from Dahl, *(b)* parallels to those already existing, (c) the original ones, such as: "Two hundred grams [of bread] governs life" and "We'll manage to drag ourselves through the day, but the night is ours."

Various conversational colloquialisms deviate from the usual phrase constructions—"That brigade leader is smart who presses upon the percentage norm. With it we feed ourselves." The features of the folklore style are present in descriptions—"Whether for long or for only a while, we mend all three windows with roofing felt." "The sun rose red, hazy above the empty zone: where the snow-screens of prefabricated homes were covered with snow, where the beginnings of a stone wall.". . . A folkish type of comparison—"They surrounded the stove, as if it were a woman; they all crept up to hug it."

Intonations, rhythms, and interruptions typical of *skaz* spring up as if to reflect the very breathing of the narrator:

> It was just as he expected, and everyone else expected it too. If there were five Sundays in the month, they gave you three and sent you to work on the other two. It was just as he expected, but when he heard it his soul became cramped and distorted. Who is not sorry about the loss of a sweet Sunday?

In summary, the vocal image of a storyteller is merged with the traits of a simple worker with a hard life. The reader readily identifies this storyteller with Ivan Denisovich himself.

This dual image of the narrator is nowhere split by the grammatical "I." On the contrary, in certain places the concept of "we" (understood in Russian) is emphasized.

> . . . The number spells nothing but trouble for *us*.

> The thirty-eighth, of course, wouldn't let any stranger near their stove. . . . Never mind, *we'll* sit here in the corner. It's not so bad.

"Mo-ortar," echoes Shukov. . . . *We* have to pull the string to a higher row. Forget it, *we'll* lay one row without a string.

Who is included in this "we" along with Ivan Denisovich? Of course, the author himself is reincarnated in the hard-working narrator. The last quote, which deals with stone masonry is, moreover, an autobiographical confirmation of this—Solzhenitsyn worked as a stone mason in the prison camp at Karanda.

This reincarnation creates a mode of exceptional vocal richness. Who indeed would attribute this knowledge of Dahl's dictionary, this aphoristic judgment, this generous speech imagery, to a *kolkhoz* [collective form] storyteller? In this mode two "carriers of the author's appraisal" seem to merge, and the language of both is based on the folk idiom.

The process of reincarnation—the transition from a literary or written style to a spoken, colloquial one—is easy to trace. Here is a segment; the *skaz* style is set off from the "written" by italics.

> The squads sat at the table or pressed closely together in the aisles, they were waiting for seats to become available. Shouting above the crush, two or three men from each squad were carrying bowls of stew and oatmeal on wooden trays and trying to find room for them on the tables. *And anyway, he doesn't hear, this stiff necked idiot! There, he bumped the tray! Splash, splash! You have a hand free—hit him on the neck, on the neck! That's it! Don't stand there blocking the way, looking for something to swipe.*

The author's immersion in the spoken manner of a prison camp worker is the very basis for the illustration of Ivan Denisovich's "one day" *from within,* about which Lakshin wrote. It is the nature of the emotion and expressiveness contained in the illustration.

Turning to an oral *počvennost'* style establishes the story's tonal directness and sincerity, which charms the reader. This tonality proves to be, at the same time, both an aesthetic element because it precludes verbosity, and with the absolute compactness of its literary expression it imparts to a cursory observation or to the minutest details an almost symbolic depth and significance.

The simplicity and confidentiality of the story give a visual quality, a luminescence, to the scenes—in the barracks, the mess hall, the search areas, in the construction of TEC (Technical Electric Stations), in the plasticity and colorings of Buinovsky, Tzesar, Fetiukov, and others from Shukov's environment.

And most of all, the character of Ivan Denisovich himself. Perhaps only a line—"Then Shukhov took his hat from his shaved head, no matter how cold it was he could not allow himself to eat with his hat on . . ."—conveys to the reader Ivan Denisovich's inner comeliness, which has inspired critics to associate him with Tolstoy's Platon Karataev.

The simplicity and sincerity of the narrative style, found in the folk quality of language, is extended by Solzhenitsyn to other of his structurally more complicated works.

CHAPTER 4

Politics and
One Day

One Day's Publication Was a Political Decision

Zhores A. Medvedev

Even before *One Day* was published in *Novy Mir*, the literary journal supervised by the Central Committee of the Communist Party, Zhores Medvedev, a famous geneticist, had already heard about the book. He notes that Solzhenitsyn had written the novel between 1956 and 1958, but found the courage to submit it for publication in 1961, after official pronouncements on the abuses of the Stalin era had begun to surface. Although Nikita Khrushchev found the novel politically useful, he had to work hard to get it approved by the Communist Party. Medvedev himself was imprisoned in a mental institution in 1970, but was released after local and international supporters loudly protested.

By September 1964 I knew a great deal about Solzhenitsyn, although at that time I had not yet met him. I had a special interest, which was partly personal, in his fate, in his writings, and in all the circumstances connected with their publication, so that I was an attentive follower of all the events surrounding the appearance of his novel and his stories in *Novy Mir*.

His novel breached—for a time—the barrier in the path of a truly realistic literature which would lay bare the crimes of our Stalinist past. Its publication, it seemed, could only help to consolidate the democratic process. It encouraged hope that in its wake other writings—polemical, historical or scientific—would find their way into print, works that would not attempt to ignore the experiences of the past. *One Day in the Life of Ivan Denisovich* was therefore seen not only as marking a new stage in the development of Soviet literature but also as a sign of improvement in all aspects of in-

From *Ten Years After Ivan Denisovich*, by Zhores A. Medvedev, translated by Hilary Sternberg. Copyright © 1973 by Zhores A. Medvedev. Reprinted by permission of Alfred A. Knopf, a division of Random House, Inc.

tellectual life in [Soviet] society. Solzhenitsyn's success aroused great hopes in other people, myself included, who had completed works which, for political reasons, had not seen publication.

It was because of my book on [the Soviet biologist] Lysenko and his followers that I learned of Solzhenitsyn's novel long before it was published in *Novy Mir*. In the summer of 1962 some friends of mine had told members of the staff of *Komsomolskaya Pravda* of the first version of my work. There was strong support for the typescript in the editorial office and I was commissioned by the science department to write an article on the prospects for Soviet genetics. The article was written jointly by myself and the Leningrad geneticist V.S. Kirpichnikov. To ensure its publication editors decided to acquaint some prominent scientists and writers with the work on which it was based. . . .

I took my article on the prospects for Soviet genetics to *Novy Mir*. It was there that I first heard about a story of labor-camp life by an unknown author from Ryazan. The story was said to be of exceptional literary merit and one of the *Novy Mir* staff put it to me that since the novel had only recently been brought to the attention of [Nikita] Khrushchev, it would be better if I did not further embarrass *Novy Mir* by inquiring into other questions that might irritate the party leader. . . .

WITH BATED BREATH

My curiosity was whetted by the news of a story that described life in a camp. The writer V.A. Kaverin whom I met at that time had read it and considered it an outstanding piece of writing. He also told me that Kornei Chukovsky had called it "a literary miracle". But I did not succeed in tracking down the manuscript. I learned in October that a decision to publish the story had been taken "right at the top" and that it would come out in issue No. 11 of the journal. From that moment I watched carefully for the appearance of that issue by scanning the catalogues in the Lenin Library. Copies of books destined for the Lenin Library are received in the course of the obligatory "advance distribution" whereby the first thirty or forty copies of an edition are distributed to important institutions in Moscow. The edition proper comes out two or three weeks later. By November 9 or 10 I was reading Solzhenitsyn's *One Day in the Life of Ivan Denisovich* in the library.

I read it three times straight through; I was there all day. Never in my life had I voluntarily read the same piece of writing several times in succession.

A week later everybody was talking of Solzhenitsyn's story, and its author, and the history of the publication of this extraordinary work had become the subject of countless legends. Later on, when I had become more closely acquainted with Alexander Tvardovsky and the editors of *Novy Mir* (where the question of publishing a shortened version of my book on Lysenko was being discussed) I was to hear from [Aleksandr] Tvardovsky on several occasions accounts of some of the events that had preceded the publication of Solzhenitsyn's story. Comparing the details he gave me with what I learned from other persons connected with *Novy Mir*, I am confident that the following brief account is authentic.

Solzhenitsyn had written the story between 1956 and 1958 but made no attempt to have it published until the end of 1961, since he thought its chances were nil. Nor could he bring himself to tell literary friends in Moscow about it, even privately. However, after the Twenty-Second Party Congress openly condemned Stalin's crimes the situation was radically altered. The Twentieth Congress in 1956, too had, heard evidence against Stalin, and this had been in the form of a "secret" speech by Khrushchev which was never published. At the Twenty-Second Congress members of the Presidium of the Central Committee and other leading speakers related the dreadful details of Stalinist repressions, mass executions of Soviet citizens, and the rule of arbitrariness and violence. These speeches were published in the Soviet Press, which indicated that the party leadership had resolved to disclose to the people the whole truth about the crimes of the past.

In the new atmosphere Solzhenitsyn decided to offer his story for publication. In a speech to the Congress Tvardovsky had called upon writers to faithfully reflect the dark sides of the "cult of personality", and Solzhenitsyn paid close attention to this. At Solzhenitsyn's request Lev Kopelev and his wife Raisa Orlova took the typescript to *Novy Mir* at the end of December 1961 and handed it to a staff member in the prose section. At that stage it was called simply *SHCH — 845*, after the number which Ivan Denisovich Shukhov bore on his chest, his back and his hat. Nor was there any indication of the author's identity; Kopelev would only say that he lived in Ryazan. The typescript had an unusual appearance, for it was typed in single spacing, with almost no margins, and covered both sides of the paper. Either the author was saving on paper or else he felt that the less paper he used the more easily his writings could be stored.

TVARDOVSKY'S ROLE

Despite the unprofessional look of the typescript it was read with great interest in the prose section. The first member of the editorial staff to read it was Anna Samoilovna Berzer. At her request it was quickly re-typed by Tvardovsky's personal secretary after which Anna Berzer passed it to Tvardovsky, recommending it to his attention. Tvardovsky took the type-script home with him. Late that evening, lying in bed, he began reading it, and was so excited that he got up and dressed and sat at his desk almost till morning to read the remainder. Next day at the office he asked to be put in touch with Kopelev immediately, for the author's name and address to be tracked down and for the author to be summoned to Moscow at once.

Several meetings were held at Tvardovsky's office, and it was decided to request permission of the Central Committee to publish the story. No one on the editorial staff had any doubts that an editorial decision alone would not suffice to ensure the story's safe passage through the censor's office. The journal had just published N. Bondarev's novel *Silence,* in which there was a scene describing a house search and the arrest of a person following a slanderous denunciation by an informer. The scene was successfully retained, but with great difficulty, and its publication was followed by official reprimands.

The author of *SHCH — 854* came to the offices of *Novy Mir* at Tvardovsky's invitation and made a very good impression there. At a meeting to discuss the story it was decided to change the title; it was Tvardovsky who suggested *One Day in the Life of Ivan Denisovich.*

Before approaching the Central Committee of the Communist Party Tvardovsky decided to have the story reviewed by leading literary figures in Moscow. Copies of the manuscript were sent to K. Chukovsky, S. Marshak, A. Kaverin, the literary critic V. Lakshin and a number of other men of letters. Their opinions were most favourable.

Then Tvardovsky, and his deputy A.G. Dementiev, drafted a letter to Khrushchev. They cited the unanimous opinion of members of the editorial board and prominent literary figures within the Soviet Writers' Union; *Novy Mir*, they said, requested him to consider the matter of the story's publication.

A STORY THAT ENNOBLES

Aleksandr Tvardovsky, poet and editor of Novy Mir, *which first published Solzhenitsyn's novel, was instrumental in having the work published. He wrote the preface to the book: An excerpt follows.*

One Day in the Life of Ivan Denisovich . . . is a work of art. And it is the way in which the raw material is handled that gives it its outstanding value as a testimony and makes it an artistic document, the possibility of which had hitherto seemed unlikely on the basis of "concrete material."

In Solzhenitsyn the reader will not find an exhaustive account of that historical period marked in particular by the year 1937, so bitter in all our memories. The theme of *One Day* is inevitably limited by the time and place of the action and by the boundaries of the world to which the hero was confined. One day of Ivan Denisovich Shukhov, a prisoner in a forced labor camp, as described by Alexander Solzhenitsyn (this is the author's first appearance in print) unfolds as a picture of exceptional vividness and truthfulness about the nature of man. It is this above all that gives the work its unique impact. The reader could easily imagine many of the people shown here in these tragic circumstances as fighting at the front or working on postwar reconstruction. They are the same sort of people, but they have been exposed by fate to a cruel ordeal—not only physical but moral. . . .

The effect of this novel, which is so unusual for its honesty and harrowing truth, is to unburden our minds of things thus far unspoken, but which had to be said. It thereby strengthens and ennobles us.

The stark tale shows once again that today there is no aspect of our life that cannot be dealt with and faithfully described in Soviet literature. Now it is only a question of how much talent the writer brings to it. There is another very simple lesson to be learned from this novel. If the theme of a work is truly significant, if it is faithful to the great truths of life, and if it is deeply human in its presentation of even the most painful subjects, then it cannot help but find the appropriate form of expression. The style of *One Day* is vivid and original in its unpretentiousness and down-to-earth simplicity. It is quite unselfconscious and thereby gains great inner strength and dignity.

Leopold Labedz, "Alexander Tvardovsky's Preface to *One Day*." *Solzhenitsyn: A Documentary Record.* Allen Lane The Penguin Press, London: 1970.

SECURING KHRUSHCHEV'S APPROVAL

Tvardovsky knew Khrushchev well. However, he rejected the idea of delivering the letter in person, deciding to send it through official channels. The letter from *Novy Mir*, and with it the copy of *Ivan Denisovich*, was handed to Khrushchev's assistant V.S. Lebedev, who dealt with cultural matters. As personal assistant to Khrushchev, Lebedev was to a certain extent independent of the literature section of the Central Committee's Ideological Commission, which was headed by D. Polikarpov, a man of extremely conservative, Stalinist views.

Lebedev displayed enormous interest in Solzhenitsyn's story and went to great lengths to ensure that it would meet with a favourable reception from Khrushchev.

Ivan Denisovich was read aloud to Khrushchev by Lebedev at Pitsunda on the Black Sea coast, where he was spending his summer holiday. It was late August or early September. Khrushchev telephoned A.I. Mikoyan, who was holidaying nearby, praised the story and asked him to read it through. Mikoyan too expressed his approval. Following this the question of publishing the work was entered on the agenda of forthcoming sessions of the Presidium of the Central Committee. *Novy Mir* received an instruction to print off twenty copies, to be marked "proof copy", for the members of the Presidium of the Central Committee, and this was promptly done. (In addition Tvardovsky ordered five copies for the editorial staff, and he presented one of these to the author. In accordance with regulations, chief editors and their deputies have the right to order galley proofs and then print off a run of several bound page proofs. The censor does not read the manuscript but the printers' proof which he passes "for printing", after which the press may print the main edition.)

I have heard various theories about why Khrushchev, who liked Solzhenitsyn's story, did not issue a personal directive regarding its publication. All these theories are based on a failure to understand that there are limitations to the powers of the First Secretary[1]; these are most strictly observed, particularly where any kind of publication is concerned. Glavlit (the censorship) is a largely secret, interdepartmental organisation operating on instructions en-

---

1. Khrushchev's full title was First Secretary of the Central Committee and Chairman of the Council of Ministers of the USSR.

dorsed by the Presidium of the Central Committee, the USSR Council of Ministers and the KGB. If on the basis of such instructions Glavlit bans a particular publication, its decision can be altered only by decree of the Presidium or the Secretariat of the Central Committee. A personal directive from Khrushchev would not have sufficed to lift the censor's ban (if it was an important publication). Equally, a personal directive from Khrushchev would not have been binding on a censor about to examine the question of the publication of *Ivan Denisovich*. For whatever decision is reached by the highest authorities the proof copy of the story must still carry the censor's signature; without this the printer would not accept it to go to press. Regulations regarding the press are in fact adhered to far more strictly than the Constitution of the USSR, [particularly sections] which deal with freedom of the press, secrecy of correspondence, freedom to demonstrate, and other civil rights. In some countries the executive head of state, the President for example, is not empowered to *prohibit* the organs of the press from publishing any particular material. In the USSR the head of state has the right to *prohibit* publication and may exercise this right even after publication has been approved by Glavlit, which is why advance copies of all publications are automatically sent to the office of the First Secretary for approval. But he does *not* have the right to bypass the censor and issue direct orders for publication, just as he may not promulgate laws, edicts and decrees, or declare a state of war.

THE CENTRAL COMMITTEE'S STAMP

The first session of the Presidium of the Central Committee, at which the agenda included the question of the publication of Solzhenitsyn's story in *Novy Mir*, did not manage to reach a decision. Some members of the Presidium announced that they had not had time to read it. Others ventured cautious remarks to the effect that the camp guards ought not to have been shown in such an unfavourable light, "after all, they were only doing their duty". The matter was postponed until the next session, at which a motion in favor of publication, proposed by Khrushchev and seconded by Mikoyan, was carried unanimously.

There exist several versions of what happened at that session, but they are of dubious authenticity. The agenda of a session of the Presidium covers a multitude of diverse matters, and the publication of the story could not have been the chief, much less the sole item. One cannot therefore trust either legends that tell of a lengthy debate on the matter and of clashes between differing points of view, or rumors that the question was greeted with complete silence which Khrushchev then declared a "sign of consent". Every member of the Presidium certainly had before him a draft resolution, prepared by the Central Committee staff, which was duly passed, and this resolution of the Central Committee eventually reached the offices of *Novy Mir.* Issue No. 11 of the journal, with Solzhenitsyn's story occupying pages 8 to 74, had secured the necessary visas to "go to press". Tvardovsky arranged with the publishing-house *Izvestiya,* of which *Novy Mir* is part, to have the size of the edition increased by forty thousand copies. Furthermore, two thousand five hundred copies of the journal were ordered for the enlarged Plenary Session of the Central Committee of the Communist Party, which was to open in November and be devoted to the reorganisation of industrial and agricultural administration in the country, the most radical reform proposed by Khrushchev.

The Plenum opened on November 19, 1962. Tvardovsky, as a member of the Central Committee, was also in the Kremlin Palace of Congresses. Afterwards he would relate with satisfaction how, wherever he looked, he saw blue copies of *Novy Mir* in every hand.

Reviews of *One Day in the Life of Ivan Denisovich* were quick to appear in all the main papers. And they all expressed exalted and appreciative enthusiasm. Less than a week after the story's publication *Pravda* (November 23, 1962) carried an article entitled "In the Name of Truth in the Name of Life" which said among other things:

> Into our literature there has come a writer gifted with a rare talent . . . Solzhenitsyn's story at times calls to mind Tolstoy's artistic power in its depiction of the national character . . .

> . . . But why is it that upon reading this remarkable story not only is one's heart wrung with grief but a light penetrates one's soul? It is because of the story's profound humanity, because in it people remained people even in an atmosphere of mockery . . .

The author of this article was the literary critic Vladimir Ermilov, a conservative and an opportunist who had figured in many of the pogrom-like campaigns of the Stalin era. A real breakthrough must have occurred if a man with such a reputation now published an enthusiastic review of *One Day in the Life of Ivan Denisovich.*

A few days later TASS [Soviet news agency] circulated to all newspapers an article giving biographical information about Solzhenitsyn. The article, "A New Name in our Literature", was published on November 28, 1962, in *Moskovskaya Pravda. Sovetskaya Rossiya* and many republican and provincial papers. . . .

> Solzhenitsyn's talent was appreciated too by the USSR Union of Writers. Without waiting for Solzhenitsyn, who at that time was teaching physics in a Ryazan school, to submit an application for membership of the Writers' Union, the Union admitted him to membership on its own initiative. The Novosti Press Agency dispatched a special correspondent to Ryazan to observe Solzhenitsyn giving his lessons of the winter term.

Solzhenitsyn's Prison Experience

David Burg and George Feifer

The following essay describes the camp in Ekibastuz where Solzhenitsyn served out the final two years of his sentence. David Burg and George Feifer observe that Solzhenitsyn would soon use the prison camp as the setting for *One Day* and the numerous prisoners he had met there as characters. Burg, a writer and journalist as well as translator, wrote with Martin Page the book *The Day Khrushchev Fell* and translated with Nicholas Bethell Solzhenitsyn's *Cancer Ward* into English.

On a balmy morning in mid-May 1950, Solzhenitsyn was suddenly interrupted while clearing winter leaves from the park, and within hours found himself in transport to an unknown destination. His first leg was to a transit jail where prisoners often stayed months in severely overpopulated cells while offices of the prison empire matched the need for labor in this or that far-flung outpost against the available supply. Solzhenitsyn spent the summer of 1950 awaiting allocation, and it was again growing cold when his long migration to the camps began.

"Transport" was a distinct phase, often the most perilous, of a prisoner's life. Obsessive security during any shifting of prisoners led to search after search of their persons—in this case, after they had been stripped to their underwear in the bitter cold. Throughout their long shunting across the country, the prisoners lived in "gray transit jails with a permeating stink and sealed suffocating compartments of freight cars." The suffocation was caused by the packing of nineteen—in some cases, twenty-three—into a space designed by the tsarist penal authorities for five prisoners or one guard horse.

From *Solzhenitsyn*, by David Burg and George Feifer (New York: Stein & Day, 1972). Copyright © by George Feifer/Acc't # 1368575. Reprinted by permission of Sterling Lord Literistic, Inc.

Even in the dead of the Russian winter, the freight cars were barely heated. In place of Marfino's [his former camp] regular meat and butter, Solzhenitsyn and his traveling companions were issued—at irregular intervals—with frozen bread and a lukewarm liquid best described as prison soup. One of Solzhenitsyn's autobiographical characters mentions that at one point in transit, he was without water for forty-eight hours. "When one reads Dostoyevsky describing the horrors of life at hard labor," Solzhenitsyn has written, "one is astonished. How peacefully they served their time. In ten years they didn't face a single move."

Yet in the first days of their new "adventure" at least some of the Marfino deportees felt a kind of elation. Solzhenitsyn was not alone in having taken steps to exchange the *sharashka's* [prison] distasteful ambiguities for the straightforward challenge of the camps. Other prisoners in this position were swept with a sense of release and of pride at having assumed at least some control of their own fate in the most adverse circumstances.

> what awaited them was the taiga and the tundra, the Cold Pole of Oi-Myakon and copper mines of Dzhezkazgan. They would be faced with kicking and shoving, starvation rations of sodden bread, hospitals, and death. What awaited them was only the worst. But their inner selves were filled with peace. They were possessed by the fearlessness of men who have lost *everything*— a fearlessness difficult to attain, but solid.

Emotion of this kind led Solzhenitsyn to speak of "the true greatness of man which I had learned in prison."

Although a strain of fearlessness would endure within Solzhenitsyn and others throughout their prison years, the elation of leaving Marfino quickly evaporated in contact with the realities of "transport.". . .

> The prisoner steps into his carriage, which is coupled to the mail van. Densely barred on both sides, its interior invisible from the platform, the carriage travels with an ordinary train and in its sealed, stifling closeness transports a thousand memories, hopes and fears.
>
> Where are they being taken? This is not disclosed. What awaits the prisoner at his new destination? Copper mines? A lumber camp? Or coveted farmwork where he will manage to bake himself an occasional potato or stuff his belly with fodder-turnips? Will he be laid low by scurvy or dystrophy from his very first month on general duties? . . .
>
> Maybe he won't even arrive at his destination? Will he die of dysentery in his cattle car? Or because the train will make

time for six days without bread? Or will the guards beat him
to death with their hammers for somebody's escape? Or at the
journey's end, will they throw the prisoners' frozen corpses
like logs from the unheated goods vans?

TO AN UNINHABITED PLACE

Solzhenitsyn did arrive. As his train made its way slowly
across endless plains, furtive glimpses through crevices in
the freight car walls provided a measure of relief: the station
names indicated that they were being taken not to the tundra and its permafrost, but somewhere to the southeast.
They still did not know precisely where when, cold and
hungry, they were herded into the "cutting wind" of the
steppe at a small station. The sign informed them that they
had arrived in Dzhezkazgan, a town in western Kazakhstan,
some 1500 miles from Moscow.

Excepting the extremes of polar regions, deserts, and im-
passable mountains, this was one of the least populated areas on earth. Hundreds of miles of desolate, virtually uninhabited territory surrounded the town on all sides. It was not
for nothing that the local name for the area was "the hungry
steppe." Some twenty-five miles north along the railway line
was a second Dzhezkazgan: the camp complex. A fifty-mile
branch line cut through it to the last station, which was
named Karsakpai. The labor camps scattered along the
branch line were known collectively as Karlag. After un-
loading, Solzhenitsyn was sent to one of them, a spot in this
huge empty area that bore the name "Sandy Camp."

The *raison d'être* of the complex was copper mining. It
was pursued in conditions which years later prompted
Solzhenitsyn to grieve for his comrades, whom the ore was
"poisoning to death." He himself never worked in the mines,
and learned their human cost only through his fellow prisoners. Thanks to his work experience in the Moscow camp
four years before, Solzhenitsyn was assigned to a construction brigade. Parquet flooring had a low priority in
Dzhezkazgan; he was again an unskilled laborer here. Before the year was over, Solzhenitsyn was shuffled to another
camp within Karlag, and from there to a coal-mining complex some five hundred miles to the northeast. The third
camp, still within Kazakhstan, was called Ekibastuz.
Solzhenitsyn was to serve out the final two-plus years of his
sentence here, and make its atmosphere and living condi-

tions known to the world through the peasant's perception of Ivan Denisovich, his best-known character.

Solzhenitsyn declines to talk about the details of his camp experience, even to clarify the sequences of his several camps—matters he considers private. However, it is clear that he was in Ekibastuz early in 1951, and, although he worked there too as an unskilled laborer, he soon became a bricklayer with a crew assigned to projects within the camp complex. He has said that he is present in his tale of this camp "insofar as I myself rafted timber and laid bricks."

ONE AMONG MANY

Ekibastuz belonged to a new category of camps solely for political prisoners. In nationality, education, and social background, it was a wholly heterogeneous collection including former admirals and unskilled workers, peasants side by side with urban intellectuals. Sizable representations of nationalities recently annexed to the Soviet Union, especially Balts and West Ukrainians, were sprinkled among the main body of Russians. Many of Solzhenitsyn's fellow inmates were victims of Stalin's "social prophylaxis," a particular form of the terror. Under this policy, entire groups were arrested for what their members might do, rather than individuals for their real or imagined acts. Millions of former prisoners of war, for example, were incarcerated because the Germans might have recruited some of them as spies. Tens of thousands of students were sentenced as anti-Soviet agitators because a few had actually been caught expressing something less than favorable about Stalin. Large groups of other national minorities—Chechens, Kalmuks, and Crimean Tartars, for example—suffered similarly.

Thus Ekibastuz provided Solzhenitsyn the opportunity for intimate acquaintance with many kinds of people whom he would not ordinarily have known at any length. The extreme diversity of social backgrounds influenced his outlook and, later, his work. Having lived as a rank-and-file laborer, he became that rare intellectual who spoke about "the people" without guesses, hypotheses, or poses. It required little imagination to see things through the eyes of Ivan Denisovich, that most ordinary of Russian peasants; Solzhenitsyn had lived with his prototypes and listened carefully to them when, under stress, their reactions and emotions were stripped bare. This would become apparent not only in

Solzhenitsyn's creative writing but also in his public criticism of contemporary Russian social conditions: both would have a keen sensitivity to the mood of the nation as a whole rather than of its educated minority alone.

All the prisoners in Solzhenitsyn's camp had been sentenced as spies, saboteurs, or propagators of dangerous anti-Soviet propaganda. Actually, far less than one percent were guilty of any crime whatever, even to the extent that Solzhenitsyn himself was guilty—even under the distinctive definition of "counterrevolutionary crimes" in Soviet law. Solzhenitsyn has written wryly about one Ekibastuz prisoner who was believed to be a genuine Rumanian spy. The inmates, especially other sentenced "spies," were agog over this odd creature.

POLITICAL PRISONERS

Political prisoners were considered especially dangerous, and guarded accordingly. The camps were constructed like reverse fortresses to keep the enemy *in.* "Two powerful searchlights swept the camp from the farthest watch towers," Solzhenitsyn wrote, describing an early morning in Ekibastuz. "The border lights were on, as well as those within the camps. There were so many that they outshone the stars." Specially fortified enclosures, inaccessible to prisoners, stood inside the fortress: the so-called lockup, for extra punishment of erring inmates—"the only brick building in the camp, with a high wooden fence around it"—and the bakery, which was "protected from the prisoners by barbed wire." Thus the captives were constantly confronted with physical evidence of their masters' power and their own impotence.

Another special arrangement made clear to them that the watchful power could zero in at any moment; that no one could hope for anonymity in the crowd of black uniforms. Each political prisoner was clearly identifiable by a letter-number designation. To the operators of his camp, Solzhenitsyn had no name: he was prisoner III-232. The letters of the alphabet stood for one thousand prisons. III, the twenty-sixth letter, indicated that Solzhenitsyn was the 26,232nd (political) prisoner in this single complex. Each prisoner wore his designation, in the form of prominent stencils on his uniform, during all waking hours. Former painters among the inmates were assigned the special duty of renewing the stencils.

Apart from the calculated humiliation of the designation, "politicals" lived under special restrictions such as the one which limited them to sending two letters a year. Compared to ordinary camps the discipline was stricter and the work more exhausting. Solzhenitsyn's camp, however, was not one of the worst, certainly not in comparison to those in the northern tundra. And it had the great advantage of not including professional criminals.

MIXED WITH CRIMINALS

Most ordinary camps had a mixed criminal-political population. There, as in transit jails, thieves and bandits added enormously to the politicals' hardships. Tightly organized on the principle of all for one and one for all, professional criminals mercilessly exploited and terrorized the atomized mass who belonged to no band. They forced others to fulfill their own work quotas, leaving them prey to death by exhaustion, hunger, and cold. . . . In short, the most vicious forms of criminal activity were practiced on the only available subjects, often with the connivance of the camps' administrations where the victims were politicals. . . .

Even without the pros, however, climate and geography made survival uncertain. Eastern Kazakhstan was largely uninhabited simply because it was uninhabitable, even by nomads. Ekibastuz lies a few miles from the Irtysh River, one of the half dozen great rivers of Siberia. The town is surrounded by steppeland "so flat," as a local resident put it, "that you can see everything for a hundred miles as if on your palm.". . . Violent snowstorms called *buran* in Russian were a particular test of endurance, as Ivan Denisovich expressed in his simple way. "When a *buran* begins to blow up in these parts . . . if you don't rig up a rope from the barracks to the mess hall, you lose your way. And if a prisoner freezes to death in the snow—well, he's only dog meat." Hard as they were, however, the storms were welcomed, for they provided respite from the hardest trial: work.

Solzhenitsyn's own writings were to become the classic portrait of life in the camps. But *One Day in the Life of Ivan Denisovich* is an account of a *good* day, and of a man accustomed to manual labor. For Solzhenitsyn and others not so trained, most days were that much harder. In winter, the work often lasted ten or eleven hours in the open; in summer, longer. Winds blew constantly over the naked steppe, intensifying both heat and cold to near the limits of tolerance. The unaccustomed effort of digging and bricklaying at raw construction sites demanded energy unreplenished by the rations, principally heavy bread, thin porridge, and soups of vegetables or fish. While work drained the prisoners' strength, hunger and exposure threatened their health. The inmates' thick cotton jackets provided scant protection against the fierce cold and inadequate relief from the dizzying heat. The thin-walled wooden barracks were also unequal to the elements; prisoners were almost permanently chilled in winter and sweltering in summer. The unprivileged caste who lived and worked "on general duties," as it was known, were called "sloggers." Solzhenitsyn joined them in late 1950.

Direct from Experience

One Day describes his living conditions with documentary precision. A former naval commander named Boris Burkovsky, who lived in Solzhenitsyn's barracks and appears in the novel as Commander Buinovsky, has said that "the general picture of camp life, as well as many details, was identical to that of the book." Burkovsky has also made clear that many of the novel's characters are in fact portraits from life. Among them are an experienced, authoritative work-crew leader, a privileged former film director, and Burkovsky himself, an idealistic Communist defiantly protesting against camp conditions. Unlike Solzhenitsyn's other "prison" novels, however, *One Day* contains no autobiographical character. For a description of Solzhenitsyn, therefore, one must turn to Burkovsky himself. Solzhenitsyn, he has recalled, was "a good comrade, an honest fellow." He did not stand out from the mass of prisoners, but "was taciturn [and] never got involved in loud discussions." There was no intimacy, little security, and no energy for Marfino's throbbing talk.

Like his appearance, Solzhenitsyn's mental attitude did not stand out sharply from that of many other prisoners. The advancing exhaustion of "general duties" brought him near to exasperation and despair. In accordance with his fundamental principle "not to overdo the horrors of prison life," *One Day* does not record the full extent of his desperation. Solzhenitsyn's intention was to portray "something more frightening—the gray routine year after year when you forget that the only life you have on earth is destroyed." But this decision about what to stress belonged to a later period. While on general duties in Ekibastuz, Solzhenitsyn saw himself as a kind of draft animal being worked to death, heaving a "powerless pickax" to spark against the frozen earth. He shared with other prisoners the certainty that time had stopped and his suffering would be endless. . . .

WRITING IN SECRET

Nevertheless, Solzhenitsyn was distinguished from other prisoners by his covert creativity. . . . A new kind of creative urge seized him, almost compulsive in its intensity.

Solzhenitsyn's 'writing" in Ekibastuz was in fact not quite that, for had the camp authorities suspected that one of the "drudges" was bearing witness to camp conditions he would have been locked up for long spells in the freezing isolation chamber, after which a second sentence for anti-Soviet agitation would surely have followed. Therefore his creative instinct had to be secret, together with its products. Constant searches of prisoners' persons and belongings precluded normal writing. To others in the barracks, even friends such as Commander Burkovsky, all that could be noticed of Solzhenitsyn's literary inclinations was a highly developed interest in language, something understandably rare among prisoners on general duties. In keeping with his old habit, Solzhenitsyn took pains to study the speech and social manners of his diverse collection of fellow inmates. And Burkovsky recalled that in his spare moments, Solzhenitsyn would often "lie down on his bunk to read a ragged copy of Dahl's dictionary [the Russian Webster, Littré, or Duden], jotting down things in a large notebook."

None of these jottings, however, contained anything faintly incriminating. The camp offered but one secure place for his compositions, the same place that kept the core of his existence secure. For years, Solzhenitsyn retained in the manner of the folk bards of preliterate nations. In other words, he wrote nothing but poetry and kept everything in his head.

Contrary to widespread legend, Solzhenitsyn did not compose and edit in his head: one of his old Marfino companions provided him with a safe place for writing. Transported together, they were delivered by coincidence to the same camp, where his companion was in time put in charge of its machine shop. He had Solzhenitsyn transferred from brick-laying to his work team, and found a warm safe place for his friend inside the shop. Amid the clattering of iron, unobserved by stool pigeons and guards, Solzhenitsyn rewrote his verses until satisfied, committed the day's work to memory, and destroyed the paper. Solzhenitsyn, memorized thousands of lines, some of which he occasionally recited to this man and several other trusted inmates. The prisoners were proud that they had a writer of great stature in their midst.

Readers' Responses to *One Day*

Aleksandr Solzhenitsyn

In the following survey, based on letters received by Aleksandr Solzhenitsyn after the publication of *One Day*, the novelist reproduces comments made by former prisoners, camp guards, and camp administrators, among others. Former prisoners welcomed the book and showered it with praise. Soviet officials, especially those who served in the camps, expressed criticism, denial, and sometimes, revulsion.

These are letters that I shall keep. They will be precious not only to me. Our fellow-countrymen too seldom have the opportunity to express their views on social questions; this applies even more to former prisoners. They have already been disillusioned, deceived, too many times, but all the same, this time they believed that the age of truth was beginning, and that they could write for themselves. And it was as if a common cry went up. (And they have, of course, been deceived, for the nth time. . . .)

Well, there were some who were careful. As one wrote: "I am not giving my name because I am watching my health for the remaining days of my life."

Others were even more careful—they did not write at all (after all, one can be traced from one's handwriting, it has often happened here; it's easy enough).

I think it is appropriate to leaf through these letters: from this reception given to the first scanty, muffled account of the camps we can measure what will happen when the truth is revealed in its entirety.

FORMER PRISONERS READ *ONE DAY*

When former prisoners learned from the fanfares in all the newspapers that some story about the camps had appeared,

From the Introduction to *Solzhenitsyn: A Documentary Record*, rev. ed., edited by Leopold Labedz (London: Allen Lane The Penguin Press, 1974). Copyright © Leopold Labedz, 1970, 1974. Reprinted by permission of Penguin Books Ltd.

and that the newspaper men were vying with each other to praise it, they decided unanimously: "More lies! They've managed to lie, even about this!" That our newspapers, with their usual lack of restraint, should suddenly begin to praise the truth—this really did seem inconceivable! Others did not even wish to see the work.

But in the end they find out.

Markelov: "Ivan Denisovich? That's me, sz-209. And I can give all the characters real names, not invented ones. Which camp? Ukhta, 29th encampment. Or Steplag, Balkhash, 8th section."

Mumrikov: "It's the No. 8 mine in Vorkuta."

N.A. Ivanov from Cherepovets: "We were in the 104th brigade with you, lived in the same hut."

Voichenko: "Solzhenitsyn has not even changed Tyurin's name. I knew him, and worked in the 104th brigade . . . I remember equally well the senior guard, Ivan Poltor, from the western Ukraine, always on the make, he was. He was a big fellow with black eyes that bulged frighteningly. His real name was Burdenyuk . . . I shall never forget the disciplinary officer, Sorodov, introduced in the story as Volkovoi. He did not walk round the compound, he strode majestically in a short leather coat, in smart new felt boots (made by a prisoner)—quite a picture! . . . I also knew Shukhov under another name. There was one like him in every brigade."

F.V. Shavirin: "Reading your story and comparing it with the camp, it is impossible to distinguish one from the other. . . .

B.D Golitsin: "In the story I was first of all looking for things that rang false, or were made up by the author—and I did not find one."

S.M. Rudkovsky: "One can see that you yourself were in a camp."

Posya also recognizes himself in Shukhov: "I wore the number A-691 for ten years because I was imprisoned by the Germans for two days, and I did not even see any Germans."

And another correspondent recognizes himself in Captain Buynovsky. "The captain suffered because of a gift—I suffered because of a letter from the USA. I was dismissed from service in the navy; there was discrimination against me everywhere, even in my personal life."

Rudkovsky: "Read it through with difficulty—I was there myself."

Belsky: "I could not sit still. I kept leaping up, walking about and imagined all those scenes as taking place in the camp I myself was in."

Zarin: "When I read it, I literally felt the blast of cold as one leaves the hut for inspection."

Voichenko: "Reading it my hands trembled."

Kravchenko (Yakutiya): "Now I read and weep, but when I was imprisoned in Ukhta, for ten years I shed not a tear."

P.V. Sharapov (Barnaul): "Although I wept when I read it, I felt myself a citizen with full rights among other people. Up to then I felt their chilly glances and they reminded me of Pechora and Norilsk."

E. Ya. Zaitseva: "I got it only for New Year's night!"

Svetlana Lesovik: "I am only a nurse, and there were professors and university teachers in the queue for the book. But . . . I [knew] someone in the library. . . . It seemed as if you were writing about the camp I was in."

Mark Ivanovich Kononenko: "In Kharkov I have seen all kinds of queues. . . . But I cannot remember a queue as long as the one for your book in the libraries . . . I waited six months on the list and to no avail. By chance I got hold of it [and I read it in] forty-eight hours."

Olga Chavchavadze: "After reading it, the only thing left to do is to . . . hang oneself." (She was not in prison herself—her husband perished.) And a young female student, both of whose grandfathers perished *there*—"I flicked through it."

Kaidanov from Debaltsevo: . . . "My own life is described here exactly . . . A loudly dressed lady with a gold ring said, 'I don't like this story, it's too depressing'. I answered her, 'It's better to have a bitter truth than a sweet lie'."

G. Benediktova: "It has so much life, so much pain that one's heart might stop beating. People who have not been there exclaim in horror, even say that those who informed on others should be arrested.". . .

M.I. Kalinina also gave it to various other people to read. "A teacher at the kindergarten read it avidly, and was shaken to the core, but the head of the kindergarten, a middle-aged Party member, said, 'Hm, just a lot of swearing'. Young workers at evening classes seized the chance to read it;". . .

V.I. Zhukov was sentenced back in 1941 for "terrorist acts against Stalin", [then] lost his family, possessions and apartment. He did not even read *One Day* itself, but [after] a review in *Ogonyok,* [he] made up his mind to write and ask for rehabilitation! (Through ignorance he did not realize that he could have had it long ago.) He wrote to the Prosecutor-General's office and soon received it.

G.F. Polev: "Can the time be coming when people are beginning to find out?"
Anna Matveyevna Lukyanova (Yaroslavl): "It is a joy to realize that Shukhov's dreams—'We will live through everything, may God grant an end to it'—have come true."
Shavirin: "We hope that this story is a forerunner of others. Let it be painful and bitter, as long as it is the truth!"
I. Dobryak: "This story has opened the eyes of many people to whom we were a mystery."
Lilenkov: "Truth has triumphed, but too late. The Far East and Siberia were created by unjustly condemned men who

---

1994: END OF EXILE

After 20 years of exile, Solzhenitsyn regained his citizenship and returned home. However, because of the length of years that he had been away and the changes occurring in his country, reception by the Russian people was uncertain.

On Friday, May 27, 1994, Solzhenitsyn, now 75, and his family will fly to the Far Eastern port of Vladivostok and work their way across seven time zones to Moscow. In the newspaper *Izvestia* last week, his wife, Natalia, described the trip as the fulfillment of his "destiny.". . .

The question, as argued out in the pages of several newspapers [in Moscow], is whether, 20 years after leaving Russia—which, given all its changes, would resemble 100 years after leaving most other countries—his voice will carry much influence.

"If he had returned in 1985, he could have claimed a role as political leader. Now he's just late for the plane," said Alexander Minkin, a political columnist. "It will be very hard on the old man."

Solzhenitsyn's books no longer sell well here. His latest three-part historical novel, *Red Wheel,* which he spent his entire exile writing, has not even been published in book form, appearing only as excerpts in journals. Even many of his admirers admit they could not finish it. "It's too long and too boring," said Natasha Perova, editor of the literary magazine *Glas.*

perished on the construction sites."

P.N. Ptitsyn: "Our people, guilty of nothing, reduced to the situation of the lowest of cattle, threw themselves . . . into this work . . . And when they had finished the task (bridge, tunnel, road, palace, aerodrome) they lay dying on sack-cloth. . . ."

Sushikhin, military engineer: "Some critics mock Ivan Denisovich for doing menial jobs to earn extra money. I, however, who have two higher degrees, but had no parcels or money, had to repair fountain pens, compose applications. . . ."

N.I. Ryabinin: "People, brought to total physical and moral exhaustion, perished in the hundreds of thousands. Those, however, who exercised this tyranny, in the majority of cases did so in full consciousness of what they were doing. . . ."

The journalist Girgori Amelin, in *Nezavisimaya Gazeta,* or the *Independent Gazette,* went further. "Who needs Solzhenitsyn? No one," he wrote, calling his trip "the return of a living relic to the mausoleum of all the Russias."

Yet Amelin's article inspired a full page of letters from citizens outraged at what they considered impertinence and convinced that Solzhenitsyn can be a moral compass for a nation desperately in need of one. . . .

In an interview with *Forbes* [in early May 1994], Solzhenitsyn advocated pulling in parts of Kazakhstan and Ukraine into Russian territory. He attacked Western influence on Russia, "the filth of our spiritual atmosphere" that has been brought on by the import of "pornography, drug addiction, organized crime and new types of swindles."

He decried Russia's current regime as being indifferent to "the cruel poverty and hopelessness which has afflicted the majority of the population as a result of . . . technocratic reform—after so many years of Communism, yet another heartless experiment performed on the unfortunate people of Russia.". . .

Because of the intensity of his recent invective, many here are convinced Solzhenitsyn might step into the role of a one-man opposition figure to all power and would-be power circles of post-Soviet Russia. The simple question is whether the Russian people will embrace, reject or simply nod off at his raspy lectures.

Fred Kaplan, "Solzhenitsyn's Journey Back," *Boston Globe,* May 22, 1994. Taken from boston.com, Boston Globe Online.

P.R. Martynyuk: ". . . How could it come about, that the people were in power and that [they] permitted such oppression? . . . What is described in the story is a tiny part of what I personally saw and lived through."

L. Terenteva-Mironova (Yalutorovsk) did not suffer imprisonment—she is the wife of one who died. She has a double-barrelled name because she changed it to escape persecution. "I see, I hear this crowd of hungry, freezing creatures, half people, half animals, and [among] them is my husband . . . Continue to write . . . the truth, even though they won't print it now! . . .

V.P. Tarnovsky: "And he broke up his food ration,
            And with it returned to me all Russia."

N.A. Vilenchuk: "We believed in the Party and *we were not wrong* (I spent seventeen years in the camps). We still need to have our heated arguments."

M. Kononenko: "You have described a comparatively bearable camp, not a punishment camp. From your story there is no answer to the question: why did so many never return?"

V.M. Eremenko: "I am amazed that Volkovoi allowed you to publish this story. Tell me, . . . were you never in the punishment block?"

F. Shults: "I am astonished that they have not put both you and Tvardovsky away."

We are astonished too. . .

PRISONERS STILL IN THE CAMPS READ *ONE DAY*

We talk about all this as past history, but for them it is actuality. We have served our sentences (for good?), but they are still inside. For them this story is not the whole truth, if there will be no sequel, something *about them* and the fact that things are just the same today. They want this to be said, and for something to change! If words do not lead to deeds, then what good are they? A dog barking at night in a village?

All the fuss in the newspapers about this story, calculated to impress people outside the camps and abroad, has been to the effect that "it happened, but will never happen again!" As always, they are lying about what matters most. Part of the truth has come out, but we are not allowed to go any further. And this has particularly provoked present-day prisoners.

Their letters are also a common cry. They want to know: "What about us?!"

P.A Lepekhin: "Citizen Solzhenitsyn! Help to revise the rules and administrative regulations in the penal settlements! On the basis of my letter I beg you to print in the newspaper *Izvestia* a criticism of the accursed past system."

I.G. Pisarev: "One thing I do not understand—did you want to say that *that* no longer exists or that what there was before still remains?"

A.D. Korzukhin: "The day you have described is not yet a thing of the past."

Yu. K-i: "Nothing has changed since the days of Ivan Denisovich except the external forms. A prisoner . . . he will be hurt and [feel] embittered that everything has remained unchanged."

Bratchikov: "Yesterday I read your story which is still valid at the present day. . . . People talk and write a great deal about the cult of Stalin, but what has changed if the laws about twenty-five-year imprisonment, promulgated under him, are still in force?"

V.D. Ch-n and others: "Why are people like the disciplinary officer Volkovoi still unpunished. People like [him] are [now] working as 'educators' in corrective penal institutions.". . .

V.I. Knyaginin: "Probably there is no one who could write about the present time."

A joint letter from Ust-Nera: "For us now it is considerably worse (than in the story). We are not beaten, but the guards like to say that we should be exterminated. . . . In December 1962 (when the story appeared) out of 300 men in our camp there were 190 suffering from malnutrition."

V.E. Milchikhin: ". . . You . . . were allowed to receive parcels, and to earn extra bread. We . . . receive 700 grams and no parcels . . . Nowadays you writers are discovering the injustices of the days of Beria. But why does not one of you touch on the life of non-political prisoners?". . .

Lepekhin: "Prisoners' complaints to the higher judicial organs are consistently rejected. After all, if one goes into a case and releases someone, then one is liable to be dismissed oneself." (There is definitely some truth here. Not of course justice, but self-preservation is the most important goal of the present legal system.)

Yu. K-i: . . ."They blacken us as best they can in order to justify their own existence and to show that they have a difficult task too. From the meanest guard right up to the camp boss, all have a vital interest in maintaining the existence of the camps.". . .

THE OTHER SIDE: CAMP GUARDS READ *ONE DAY*

What are "practical workers"? It turns out that this is how camp guards style themselves. The description is priceless; we had not heard it before.

Let us hear the other side, as is only proper. More precisely, let us receive our directives.

Not all of these correspondents identify themselves; maybe there are some who never wore blue flashes, and whose only bunch of keys belongs to his apartment, but they are all of one mind, all of the same ilk. They are the people whose pictures are never in the papers, but who wield the power. (One of them—S.I. Golovin—says he is a former prisoner. We must believe him.)

They are not victimized for reading this book, they have time to read it, to take notes, break it down point by point.

About Shukhov
Ivan Denisovich is a boot-licker. As a prisoner of the Germans he would be able to earn his bread; though he might have been killed by fellow prisoners (*Oleinik*, Aktyubinsk).

I do not want heroes like that—all stomach and no brain (*Pastukhova, T.S.*, Bogordsk).

The principal character of the story, Shukhov, is shown negatively, like all the others, who, as the story shows, disorganized life in the camp *(Grigorev, A.I.* Monino, Nelidovsk rainon, practical worker). . . .

You feel neither sympathy nor respect for Shukhov, nor do you feel any particular anger at the injustice done to him. (*Yu. Matveyev,* Moscow. He very likely lives with his family.). . .

All he hopes for is the sick-bay. After all, he is in a corrective labor camp. Even if he is innocent, he ought to set an example to the others, like a good Soviet citizen. . . . (*Zakharova, A.F.,* worked for the MVD since 1950, Lesogorsk, Irkutsk oblast).

Shukhov was rightly condemned. At the interrogation *no one could force him,* after all it was not 1937. He . . . was afraid of going back to the front (*V.I. Silin,* Sverdlovsk, practical worker).

Vladimir Dmitrievich Uspensky from Moscow attacks Shukhov in the greatest detail of all. (He is either an investigator or a camp administrator.) Disregarding the text of the story as obviously false testimony, he makes his case against Shukhov absolutely in the spirit of *those days:*

> Shukhov is not ill, since he could work today. But he is afraid for his health, and so rushes off to the medical orderly!

> The only place he did a decent job of work was on his own log cabin; everywhere else he is a sloppy worker.

> He never shares anything with anyone; he is a fully qualified, resourceful and merciless jackal. He is a total egoist, living only for his belly. He brings a knife into the camp in order to sell it, and a man is killed with it.

> He was the first to put up his hands and hastened to give himself into captivity, he is a real traitor to his country.

In a word, ten years is too little for Shukhov. He should have received four times that!

About Camp Regulations

Why give someone who does not work a lot to eat? His strength will remain unspent . . . Prisoners were dressed *according to the season,* and were fed no worse than the free labor force . . . The criminal world is still treated too gently (*Sergei Ivan. Golovin,* Tselinograd, served ten years).

How dare you slander camp regulations . . . ? In the camps there is less abuse than in any other Soviet institution?! (Patriotically said.) . . . Things have grown *more severe* in the camps now (*Karakhanov,* foreman). . . .

Nowadays . . . the guards always walk with sub-machine guns at the ready, and at a fixed distance go men with dogs. As regards the food, . . . it must not be forgotten that *they are not at a resort.* For this reason they must redeem their guilt by honest toil (senior official *Bazunov,* Oimyakon, fifty-five years old, veteran of the camp service).

How is it possible to discontinue body searches when prisoners try to take out of the camp letters . . . attacking the . . . Party and the Soviet government? . . .

(About the whip.) We all know . . . that corporal punishment was abolished . . . with the coming of Soviet power . . .

Solzhenitsyn describes the working of the camp as if there was no control by the Party. . . . Party organizations existed and directed all activities as conscience required (*Zakharova*).

Once you have camps, arbitrary individual acts are possible (*P.A. Pankov*).

About Informers

According to Solzhenitsyn, if one of the prisoners who is more conscious of his duties tells something to the authorities, then it is "self-preservation at someone else's expense". Some patriot, I must say! The Soviet people should say only thank you to this prisoner who has come to a proper understanding (*Zakharova*).

How informers are murdered is described as if it were a good thing. Everyone knows what an informer is. In the Soviet Union *these* people are respected, because they are progressive, politically aware people, who help to bring into the open the enemies of Soviet power. . . .

About the Guards

This story insults soldiers, sergeants and officers of the Ministry for the Preservation of Public Order [MOOP, now MVD]. The people are the creators of history, but how are the people represented [as] soldiers, sergeants and officers? They are [portrayed] as "parrots" [camp slang for sentries], blockheads, idiots in greasy field shirts and torn greatcoats (*Bazunov*). . . .

The people have glorified our heroic Soviet troops, but Solzhenitsyn makes them into "parrots". . . And what would happen if the camp guards stopped doing their work! How the people would suffer!? (*Zakharova*).

The keeping of prisoners in camps *is not a result of the cult of personality*, but is due to the carrying out of sentences . . .* The security officers are called "godfather"—a term used only by a few bad characters among the prisoners. . . (*Grigorev, A.I.*).

The security forces did not know why people were put inside[†] (*Karakhanov*). . . .

Living in remote places, [we] are deprived of all elementary human conditions. . . . [Sometimes,] we do not have enough to eat(!) . . . We are working with the rejects of society, we carry the most difficult burden for the good of the . . . people. So why are our names besmirched? . . .

In Ozerlag, to my knowledge, there was no thieving.[††] But he calls everyone a thief (*Zakharova*).

And why be displeased that the convicts are building houses, for free people to live in? (*Bazunov*).

---

* "We only carried out orders", "We did not know".
† Very significant testimony. Present-day convicts say the same.
†† Perhaps this is why there was such a careful search for letters at the exit?

About the Author Himself

You, who are not in a fit state to stand firmly an your feet (?), trample honest Soviet people into the dirt . . . You have tackled a good subject in a spirit that is not quite pure . . . Why (in the story) does no one protest at the practice of bribery? It is repulsive to Soviet man. Or did you *yourself* get your freedom with the aid of a bribe? (*Oleinik*).

You are a wet blanket, comrade Solzhenitsyn; we cannot sense in you any faith in the new life (*Kamzolova*).

Spite has clouded the gaze of . . . Solzhenitsyn, and so he cannot take a sober view of his surroundings. He thinks that only his petty personality, soured by spineless malice, is typical in literature. . . . (*N.D. Marchenko*, st. Udelnaya).

He deliberately incites the people against the organs of the MVD . . . And why is he allowed to mock the people who work in MOOP? *It is a disgrace!* (*Zakharova*).

Hear that! A disgrace! It was alright to torment people in camps for forty years, but to publish a story about it is a disgrace!

Finally, and more broadly: *the philosophical approach.*

You wish to infect Soviet man with these sores from the past (*Oleinik*).

History never has any use for the past (!!)—least of all the history of socialist culture (*A. Kuzmin*).

We paid too dearly for Soviet power to allow its activities to be debased (*Golovin*).

I would not have published this. For what reason and for whom is it? One tries to conceal one's own shortcomings instead of advertising them. We need neither sympathy nor charity (*Modne*).

Criticizing the cult of personality is necessary and inevitable. . . . It is not, however, necessary to drag in people who are not involved . . . This authority of MOOP has been . . . undermined . . . and cannot now be restored . . . (*Zakharova*).

Why do we have to make a big fuss over what was done during the personality cult? The unmasking of illegal acts is like an epidemic; writers and poets are trying to kick a dead lion . . . Perhaps Stalin and his toadies invented the class enemy as well? . . .

Do you hear that, Russia,
On our consciences
There is not a single spot! (*Anon.*)

Once again that wretched *Anon!* One would so much like to know whether he shot people himself, or only sent them to their death, or whether he is just an ordinary orthodox citizen.

And here at last is a more comprehensive historical view, the first scientific explanation of all our misfortunes:

> After the original (?) slogan, "the son is not responsible for his father", the shattered remains of the privileged classes strove to insinuate themselves into every part of the Soviet system, never abandoning thoughts of revenge for the privileges they had lost. They were particularly active in 1937(!).* They collaborated in the police forces of the enemy in 1941; from their very first day in the army, they shouted, "Everyone for himself!", and led others after them into captivity (*Pankov*).

Now we know at last it was the class enemy that decimated the Party, and let Hitler get as far as Stalingrad, only then handing over to our brilliant generals and the wise Generalissimus.

This is what is frightening—this is the way they write history . . .

(*Survey,* No. 74/75, Winter/Spring 1970)

---

* i.e. the day after the "original" slogan they had all already seized the NKVD and established their authority over the Party.

Solzhenitsyn Comments on His Work

Aleksandr Solzhenitsyn, interviewed by Nikita Struve

In the following interview with Nikita Struve, Solzhenitsyn bares his ideas on the role of the writer, how his prison experience affected his writing, and the great Russian writers who influenced him most. Even in his youth, Solzhenitsyn had dreamed of writing about the Russian revolution. Years in prison slowed his progress, but even while in prison he gathered materials, committing images and characters to memory. After he was released, he set out to transform his vision into reality, writing one book after another. Struve was a professor of Russian literature at the University of Paris at the time of writing. Also an editor and journalist, he has written several studies, including *Christians in Contemporary Russia.*

Ever since the speeches you gave in America and England, you are constantly being referred to as a political figure, whereas in fact those speeches were more of a hindrance to your creative work, were they not?

Yes indeed. It's quite striking how, for some reason, everyone who talks to me tries to draw me into politics: it's always my political views that they particularly want to hear. It upsets me very much, but that's the way it is. One reason is, of course, that Russian literature as a whole has traditionally been highly sensitive to social issues . . .

After all, your vocation from the outset, from childhood almost, was to become a writer . . . .

Yes, it is true, oddly enough: ever since the age of eight or nine I have had a notion that I must become a writer, even though I had no idea at that time how this might come about.

And how did you become a writer?

In a serious way—not until I was in prison. I tried my

From Aleksandr Solzhenitsyn, "An Interview on Literary Themes with Nikita Struve, March 1976," in *Solzhenitsyn in Exile: Critical Essays and Documentary Materials,* edited by John B. Dunlop, Richard S. Haugh, and Michael Nicolson (Stanford, CA: Hoover Institution Press, 1985). Copyright © 1985 by the Board of Trustees of the Leland Stanford Junior University. Used by permission of the publisher.

hand at writing even before the war; as a student, I really made an effort and did produce things. But this was not serious writing. I simply did not have the necessary experience. During my years in prison, I began to write in earnest. It had to be done in a truly conspiratorial fashion: the very last thing I could afford to do was to let them find out I was writing! I used to memorize things, learn them by heart—first poetry, then, later, prose as well.

That was in prison, but in the camp your writing became more ambitious . . .

Well, prison and camp—they're more or less the same thing . . .

It was in the camps, though, that your long narrative poem really took shape . . .

In effect, I kept working away at it throughout my years in the camps, then I went on to plays. I couldn't just drift along without trying to get something done. The years were passing by. But the novel, my big novel, the epic which I had thought up as early as 1936—that I could not begin to write in the camp. It was out of the question. All I could do was gather material, think things over, question eye-witnesses. In this sense, camp existence swung me around. On the one hand, it seemed to be leading me away from the central theme I wanted to work on—the history of our revolution. On the other hand, it turned out to be God's wish, as they say, for the camp experience was the ideal preparation for that other theme, which really *was* the main one. . . .

You postponed working on this project, and began writing novels during your exile in Kazakhstan.

That's not quite right: I *never* postponed it. For me the greatest, most intensely interesting aspect of camp life was the opportunity it gave me to question people who knew something about the revolution. So I kept accumulating material, even though I had no opportunity to make notes. . . . So I spent all those years memorizing facts and details, then I was set free. But by "freedom" I mean internal exile—practically the same thing as prison—and there, too, it was impossible to do any writing, for I was under surveillance and could expect my quarters to be searched at any minute.

But, even so. . . .

The prison theme was pressing so hard on me that I just had to work on it. And then I came down with cancer. This fatal disease and the book *Cancer Ward* also demanded their share of my time and energy. And that's how I finished up putting off my main subject for thirty years, and working instead on the prison and camp themes. I wrote about the *sharashka* [prison], about the cancer ward. I just couldn't fight my way through to my own theme. Then came *Gulag.* The publication of *Ivan Denisovich* put me in an extraordinary position. Hundreds of people sent me their personal recollections of life in the camps. I had to listen to them, assemble all this material, and rework it. That is when I began putting *Gulag* together.

You became a "writer of the people."

I became the accredited chronicler of labor camp life, one to whom people brought the whole truth. And these distractions continued until 1969, so that for thirty-three years I had been living my theme without ever being able to do any real work on it. Not till 1969 could I give myself fully to this, my main project.

But you came to the novel as a form while you were still in exile in the fifties. How did this happen?

To begin with, I think that every writer has his own preferences, in architectural terms, for miniatures, or for huge edifices. But, in addition, life exerts its own pressures. The material that comes our way demands that we write about it, and dictates the appropriate form. Thus, it took a combination of personal inclinations and the exigencies of the material itself, and in the case of *Gulag* the material combined with my predilection for large forms. However, my novels are not exactly examples of the small form, either: *The First Circle* and *Cancer Ward* are both a fair size.

They certainly are. . . .

Yes, but Gulag *is, in effect a part of that same story, its culmination.*

Yet the forms I had to choose were almost entirely different. This was an artistic investigation. And then there was the tactical problem of how to work up the material, these letters which had arrived out of the blue—this was all absolutely unplanned and unorganized material. Someone would come and tell me what he wanted to say, not what I happened to need. I had to break it all down into fragments, then work out where everything should go.

Isn't that rather like the way cathedrals and mosaics are built?

Well, perhaps like a mosaic. . . . In the camps, one of my

jobs was breaking up iron, heavy cast-iron objects, into pieces. They were then thrown into a furnace, mixed with metal of inferior quality, and what came out was an iron with quite different properties. I sometimes jokingly refer to my materials as lumps of iron—very high-quality iron. I lower it into the smelter, and out it comes, transformed. . . .

When you began to write your first long novels, did certain images from Russian literature pass before you or did this [their literary echoes] come about completely spontaneously? What was the guiding force, the material or the tradition?

I am guided by tradition in the sense that I read Russian literature intensively in my childhood, and it left its trace in my soul. But that is as far as it goes. While you're working, you don't think about traditions at all, and you don't think about whether you are supposed to be continuing this or that line. It simply does not occur to you. You are carried away by a new project. . . .

One never senses a smoothly flowing narrative in your works. You always want to condense, to dynamize everything static.

I just think that this compactness enables us to reveal ourselves most effectively. As in a pithy conversation, for example. But if your interlocutor is vague and boring, it makes you feel almost ill. You sense that he is talking nonsense, and your own remarks start to become dull-witted, so the whole conversation falls flat and nothing comes of it.

Does your concept of compactness operate at the lexical level, too?

Yes, down to the last phrase and the last word. It has been noted that in the late Lermontov there is not a single extraneous, fortuitous word. I am not speaking of rhyme, for rhyme dictates its own requirements, but there is not a single extraneous word in the line. That is a general phenomenon, in prose as well as poetry. Yes, compactness must extend to the individual word and phrase.

Your syntax is amazingly elliptical; you make the word dynamic.

These days, I try to throw out every superfluous word. If there's any way I can do without a word, I throw it out.

But isn't there a certain danger that one might stretch the strings of the language too tight?

I don't think so. Look at Anna Akhmatova. Before her death, she said that an eight-line poem was too long for her;

four lines were all that was needed. How often do you hear something like that? In Russian classical poetry, even a twenty-line poem was never considered to be long. But Akhmatova came to the same conclusion [as I have]—it's like sculpturing from stone, constantly trimming everything down. Twelve lines is too long, eight is too long, but four lines. . . .

How do you manage to combine this sculptured quality with such extraordinary dynamism?

BATTLING LIES

Solzhenitsyn is adamant about the work of the artist—it must serve society by adhering only to Truth. In this speech, Solzhenitsyn exhorts writers to battle lies through their art.

We shall be told: what can literature do in the face of a re-morseless assault of open violence? But let us not forget that violence does not and cannot exist by itself: it is invariably in-terwined with *the lie.* They are linked in the most intimate, most organic and profound fashion: violence cannot conceal itself behind anything except lies, and lies have nothing to maintain them save violence. Anyone who has once pro-claimed violence as his *method* must inexorably choose the lie as his *principle.* . . .

The simple act of an ordinary brave man is not to partici-pate in lies, not to support false actions! His rule: let *that* come into the world, let it even reign supreme—only not through me. But it is within the power of writers and artists to do much more: *to defeat the lie!* For in the struggle with lies art has always triumphed and shall always triumph! Visibly, irrefutably for all! Lies can prevail against much in this world, but never against art. . . .

This is why I believe, my friends, that we are capable of helping the world in its hour of crisis. We should not seek to justify our unwillingness by our lack of weapons, nor should we give ourselves up to a life of comfort. We must come out and join the battle!

The favorite proverbs in Russian are about *truth.* They forcefully express a long and difficult national experience, sometimes in striking fashion:

One word of truth shall outweigh the whole world.

Aleksandr Solzhenitsyn, "Nobel Lecture," in *Aleksandr Solzhenitsyn: Critical Es-says and Documentary Materials,* edited by John B. Dunlop, Richard Haugh, and Alexis Klimoff (Massachusetts: Nordland Publishing Company, 1973).

Well, that's not really the kind of thing I can assess. I work
with my material, and all I have in mind is how to give expression to that material.

*Are you sometimes dissatisfied with what you have writ-
ten?*

When I am, I rewrite it over and over again, always trying
to condense. Take *One Day in the Life of Ivan Denisovich,* for
example. How was it born? It was just another day in the
camps, the work was hard—I was teamed with another fellow, hauling hand-barrows—and it occurred to me that the
best way to describe the whole camp world would be
through a single day. Of course, you could describe your own
ten years in the camp, the whole history of the camps—but
it was sufficient to collect everything that happened in one
day, like piecing together little fragments. . . .

In the camp?

In the camp. Of course, at that time it was insane to think
about writing it. And then the years passed. I wrote a novel, fell
ill, was dying of cancer for a while. But then, one day in—I'm
sorry, what was the year?—in 1959, I thought that now I
might perhaps be able to do something with this idea. It had
simply lain there for seven years. Well, I thought, let's try
writing about one day in the life of one *zek.* . . . I completed
One Day in the Life of Ivan Denisovich incredibly quickly and
then hid it for a long time. When I went to *Novyi mir,* they
asked me: "How long did it take you to write it?" It was impossible to admit that I had written it in little over a month,
because their next question would have been: "And what,
pray, have you been writing for the rest of the time?". . .

*Is that the way you usually work: years of gestation and
then a rapid first draft?*

You know, come to think of it, I suppose the moment *is*
sudden. Once, after I had been released from the dispensary,
I was walking about Tashkent, going to the commandant's
office, when suddenly almost the whole of *Cancer Ward*
came to me in a flash.

A primary intuition, as it were . . .

Well, at least as far as the Kostoglotov line goes; that came
to me almost complete. But I heard about Rusanov from my
neighbors in the ward. I never shared a ward with him myself, and his story-line comes from what they had to say
about him. It occurred to me at the time that this might make
a story. But once the idea had formed it just lay dormant: for

all that came of it, it might as well never have been. But in 1963, when my works had already begun to be published, I wondered what kind of thing I could write, that I could submit openly to *Novyi mir.* And that is how I came to write *Cancer Ward.* I might as easily not have done so; it could have gone on lying there. And if something had distracted me, I might never have written *Ivan Denisovich* either.

Or was it perhaps something that you would eventually have needed to write?

No. I have plots which have never been written up. There is just the initial concept, a few words jotted down, and that is as far as it will go.

So they will never be written?

I'm afraid not, because my main theme is driving me on, and there is little enough time left in my life as it is. . . .

You have mentioned Ivan Denisovich. Many people might think that there is an autobiographical element here, but in reality this is a composite image , is it not?

It can't be helped, I really cannot envisage any higher task than to serve reality—i.e., to recreate a reality which has been crushed, trampled and maligned. And I do not consider imagination *(vymysel)* to be my task or goal. I have not the slightest desire to dazzle the reader with my imaginative powers. Imagination is simply a means by which the artist can concentrate reality. It helps to concentrate reality—and that is its only role.

Reality being so rich. . . .

When I hit on the idea of describing a day in the life of one zek, it was, of course, clear that he would have to be one of the most lowly rank-and-file members of the army of Gulag. I made a mental note of the project, but it evolved no further, and when I undertook to write it in 1959, the question was —whom should I pick? I had rubbed shoulders with very many prisoners in my time; I could recall dozens and dozens whom I had known very well, hundreds even. For some reason, the figure of Ivan Denisovich suddenly, and quite unexpectedly, began to take shape. First the surname —Shukhov—came to me quite by chance. I did not choose it; in fact it was the name of one of the soldiers in my battery during the war. Then, together with the surname, came his face and a few real-life details—the area he was from, and the way he spoke. And all at once, this private from a battery in the Soviet-German war began to take his place in the story *(povest')*, even though he had never been imprisoned. Of course, there was a similarity, in that he, too, was just one of the rank and file, only in different circumstances. But Ivan Denisovich's biography—how he ended up in the camp, and how he behaved when he was there—was drawn from people I met in the camp. I didn't get that from the real Shukhov, who, after all, was never inside. . . .

Might it not be more correct to speak of experience than "autobiographical" factors?

Yes, indeed, experience . . . personal experience. . . . Because without personal experience, of life or of human psychology, it is impossible to write at all. Why is it that young people cannot instantly become writers? Because experience is precisely what they lack. If I set out to describe you, then my task is to enter into you as deeply as I can, and to communicate you to others. But that is impossible if I haven't yet gained any practical experience of human psychology. . . .

The fact that you have, in a sense, rejected the short form seems to indicate a certain tendency to synthesize . . . the experience of Russian history, [and] to achieve a formal synthesis by combining various literary devices.

It is not that I have rejected the short form. It would give me a lot of satisfaction—artistic satisfaction—to have a rest and go back to the short form.

But you cannot permit yourself to do so?

No. Unhappily, the course of Russian history has been such, that in the sixty years which have elapsed since the events I am describing, not one substantial, coherent *literary* account has been written, nor a documentary one, for that matter. The last eyewitnesses are dying off, but it is still possible to question some of the living. The whole fabric of life as it existed before and up to the revolution has been destroyed, and my generation may well be the last which can still treat this material as something other than history, which can write about it not purely in the form of a historical narrative, but drawing upon the vestiges of living memory. In any case, my own childhood memory has preserved the post-revolutionary atmosphere very well. In the twenties, the population of Russia was still almost prerevolutionary in the way it lived. The breath of those times still comes to me. It helps me process the material. . . .

You have been criticized for reproducing [John] Dos Passos's method. . . .

Certainly, I learned from Dos Passos, but in a specific sense. I learned two things, if you will—his newspaper montages and his so-called camera-eye. . . . Anyway, I saw that, in their present form, these two techniques were not applicable to my project, but that they might indeed be applicable if they were modified. Take the camera-eye, for example. His camera-eye is not the same as a scenario. If you look at Dos Passos you'll find that you cannot film with his camera-eye. So, why did he call it that? These are more like lyrical fragments. . . .

Would you have been a writer under any circumstances? Have you ever thought about what you might have become . . . if you hadn't been imprisoned . . . ?

I can't even begin to imagine *normal* circumstances, but under Soviet conditions, I must say that there were great spiritual dangers confronting me if I had not been arrested at the end of the war. For, if I had become a writer in the mainstream of Soviet literature, then of course, I would not have been myself and would have lost God. It's not easy to imagine what I might have turned out to be, with all those literary projects of mine. But, luckily, fate led me through the Archipelago: the path seemed long at the time, but actually it could not have been shorter. . . .

Which figure in Russian literature—which writer—serves as your guiding star? Which writer do you feel closest to?

I think that for all of us, and for more than a century now, the guiding star is Pushkin. In fact, the further we move away from him, the more we realize how much we have lost in him, and how much of what he did needs to be continued. Pushkin is an incomparable star, in that he created our language and literature (not out of nothing, of course)—in this respect he has never had an equal. But, of course, in one way or another we have been brought up on the entire tradition of the nineteenth century. Tolstoy and Dostoevsky have always been an influence, on each and every one of us.

But at one time Tolstoy was a moral authority for you?

Rather to the contrary. I read *War and Peace* when I was ten years old. . . . I think that novel had a strong effect on me and on my desire to write an historical novel. But if we are talking about when I was older and already concerned with moral questions, then Dostoevsky poses such questions more sharply, profoundly and prophetically, and with greater relevance to the modern world.

CHRONOLOGY

1918

Aleksandr Isayevich Solzhenitsyn is born on December 11 in Kislovodsk, one year after the 1917 Russian Revolution and six months after his father's death.

1924–1936

Solzhenitsyn and his mother move to Rostov-on-Don, where Aleksandr spends most of his childhood and completes his elementary and secondary education.

1936

Solzhenitsyn graduates from high school and enters Rostov University's Faculty of Mathematics and Physics. He becomes an ardent Leninist, committed to a Russia led by the Communists.

1939–1940

Attends a correspondence course in literature at the Moscow Institute of Philosophy, Literature, and History.

1940

Marries Natalya Alekseyevna Reshetovskaya.

1941

Graduates with honors from Rostov University.

1941–1945

Enlists in the Soviet army and serves in World War II as an artillery officer.

1945

Criticized Stalin's mismanagement of the war effort in letters to his wife and a friend; he is arrested and sentenced to eight years in prison for these criticisms.

1945–1946

Serves sentence in prison camps near Moscow.

1946

In the summer, Solzhenitsyn is dismissed from the research institute and is moved to a labor camp in northern Kazakhstan, where he works as a miner, bricklayer, and foundryman; encourages his wife to marry another man to make her life easier; after much uncertainty, she agrees and moves in with Vsevolod Somov.

1953

Released from prison after serving eight years and is sent to internal exile.

1953–1954

Solzhenitsyn becomes ill with cancer; he is sent to Tashkent for treatment, where he recovers.

1953–1964

After Stalin's death, Soviet premier Nikita Khrushchev implements a policy of de-Stalinization, bringing about a period of relative cultural liberalism.

1956

Under Khrushchev, the Twentieth Communist Party Congress grants amnesty to millions of Soviet political prisoners; Solzhenitsyn is released from internal exile.

1957

In a decision of the Soviet Supreme Court, Solzhenitsyn is declared fully rehabilitated; he settles in Ryazan and remarries Natalya Reshetovskaya.

1957–1959

He starts to write *One Day in the Life of Ivan Denisovich* and to gather material for another book on the concentration camps.

1961

Writes the first volume in a cycle of histories of the events leading to the 1917 Russian Revolution, including World War I.

1962

With the help of Aleksandr Tvardovsky and the approval of Khrushchev, *One Day* is published in *Novy Mir;* in a week, thousands of copies are sold, and he becomes an international celebrity; at the same time, hostile reviews appear in the Soviet press; Solzhenitsyn gives up teaching to become a full-time writer.

1963

One Day is published in the West; "An Incident at Krechetovka Station," "Matryona's Place," and "For the Good of the Cause"—all short stories—are published in *Novy Mir;* English translations of the first two are also published in the same year; *Novy Mir* nominates Solzhenitsyn for the Lenin Prize in literature, but he does not win; hostile criticism from the Soviet political and literary establishment continues.

1964

"For the Good of the Cause" is published in English.

1965

Following the fall of Khrushchev, authorities step up attacks on Solzhenitsyn; the secret police (KGB), confiscates the manuscript of *The First Circle*, the play *Victory Celebrations*, and other personal papers; Solzhenitsyn protests the seizure.

1966

He submits *Cancer Ward* (part one) to *Novy Mir*.

1967

The first part of *Cancer Ward* is published in Czechoslovakia in January; Solzhenitsyn writes an open letter in May to the Fourth Congress of the Soviet Union's Writers' Union and denounces its policy of censorship; in September he attacks the Writers' Union, demanding that it authorize the publication of *Cancer Ward*.

1968

Novy Mir abandons *Cancer Ward*, but two volumes of the Russian-language edition are published in London and Germany in January; the first volume of the English edition is also published; the Russian language edition of *The First Circle* is published in Germany; the English edition is published in the United States in the same year; two volumes of the English edition of *Cancer Ward* are published in London; *The Gulag Archipelago: 1918–1956*, a scathing exposé of the Soviet concentration camps and terrorism, is smuggled out of the Soviet Union; *Candle in the Wind*, a play, is published in Russia; an English translation is published in 1973; Solzhenitsyn meets Natalya Svetlova, a mathematician who becomes one of his assistants.

1969

The Writers' Union expels Solzhenitsyn in November; he and his supporters in both the Soviet Union and the West protest;

The Love Girl and the Innocent, a play, is published in Russia and translated into English in the same year.

1970

Solzhenitsyn is awarded the Nobel Prize in literature; he learns that Natalya Svetlova will soon have his child; his wife tries unsuccessfully to commit suicide; she refuses to grant Solzhenitsyn a divorce.

1971

Denied publication of his work at home and worried about the possibility of deportation, Solzhenitsyn authorizes the publication of the Russian edition of *August 1914,* the first part of *The Red Wheel*—the saga of the Russian Revolution— in France; a son is born to Solzhenitsyn and Svetlova.

1972

The English translation of *August 1914* is published in the United States and England.

1973

The KGB learns about the existence of a copy of *The Gulag Archipelago;* the KGB tries to negotiate with Solzhenitsyn not to publish *Gulag,* but he refuses and authorizes the publication of the first volume of the Russian edition in Paris; he divorces Reshetovskaya and marries Svetlova.

1973–1976

Three volumes of the Russian edition of *Gulag* are published in France.

1974

The Soviet government arrests Solzhenitsyn on the charge of treason, strips him of his citizenship, and deports him to West Germany; he settles with his family in Switzerland, where they stay until 1976; the Russian edition of a volume of poetry, *Prussian Nights,* is published in France.

1974–1978

Three volumes of the English edition of *Gulag* are published in the United States and England.

1975

The Russian language edition of *Lenin in Zurich* is published in France; the English edition is published in the United States and England in 1976; the Russian language edition of

The Oak and the Calf, a memoir, is published; the English translation is published in the West in 1980.

1976–1980s

Solzhenitsyn, Svetlova, their three sons, and Svetlova's daughter from her first marriage live in Cavendish, Vermont; he continues to write and gives occasional speeches.

1977

The English edition of *Prussian Nights* is published in the West.

1978

Delivers an address at the Harvard University commencement exercises, where he criticizes the United States; the speech is published as "A World Split Apart."

1981

His play *Victory Celebrations* is published in Russia; an English translation appears in 1983.

1983

An enlarged Russian edition of *August 1914* is published.

1984

The Russian edition of *October 1916,* the second volume in *The Red Wheel,* is published in Russia; a comprehensive biography, *Solzhenitsyn: A Biography,* by Michael Scammell, is published.

1985

Soviet president Mikhail Gorbachev launches glasnost, a campaign to open Russia and start the democratization process.

1986

A single, condensed English edition of *Gulag* is published.

1986–1988

The Russian edition of *March 1917,* the third volume in *The Red Wheel,* is published in Russia.

1989

The official Soviet policy of openness (glasnost) allows the serialization of *Gulag* in *Novy Mir,* the journal that launched Solzhenitsyn's career twenty-seven years earlier; an expanded English edition of *August 1914,* retitled *The Red*

Wheel: A Narrative in Discrete Periods of Time, is published in the United States and England.

1990

His essay "Rebuilding Russia" is published; the treason charge is dropped as Gorbachev restores the citizenship of thousands of exiles, including Solzhenitsyn.

1991

The Russian language edition of *April 1917,* the fourth volume in *The Red Wheel,* is published in Russia; a supplement to *The Oak and the Calf* in Russian is published; the English edition, *Invisible Allies,* is published in the United States in 1995; meanwhile, the Soviet Union dissolves and Boris Yeltsin is elected Russian president.

1994

At age seventy-five, Solzhenitsyn returns to Russia, hoping to help in the reconstruction of his country; he starts a television program and vows to continue writing.

1996

A Grain Landed Between Two Milestones: Essays from Exile, a memoir, is published in Russia; meanwhile *What a Pity and Other Stories* comes out in the United States; Solzhenitsyn suffers a mild heart attack from which he recovers.

1997

Establishes the Solzhenitsyn Prize for Literature, funded by royalties from *Gulag.*

1998

At age eighty, he publishes a new book, *Russia in Ruin,* which criticizes the government's economic reforms; another novel, *November 1916,* the second part of the trilogy *The Red Wheel,* and a new biography, *A Century in His Life,* by English biographer D.M. Thomas, are published in the United States.

FOR FURTHER RESEARCH

Note: Solzhenitsyn's works are published in Russian and English; the publication dates stated here are those of the first English editions, unless indicated otherwise. Solzhenitsyn would often reissue, revise, and expand many of his works in later years. The list does not include stories and poems that were not translated into English, reissues, revised and expanded editions, and anthologies.

WORKS BY ALEKSANDR SOLZHENITSYN

FICTION

One Day in the Life of Ivan Denisovich (1963)

"Matryona's House" in *We Never Make Mistakes* (1963)

"An Incident at Krechetovka Station" in *We Never Make Mistakes* (1963)

"For the Good of the Cause" (1964)

Cancer Ward (in two volumes, 1968–1969; in one volume, 1970)

The First Circle (1968)

August 1914, vol. 1, the first "knot" in *The Red Wheel: A Narrative in Discrete Periods of Time* (1972); vol. 2 (1982)

The Gulag Archipelago: An Experiment in Literary Investigation: 1918–1956, 3 vols. (1974–1978); in a single, condensed volume (1986)

Lenin in Zurich (1976)

October 1916, Russian edition, 2 vols., the second "knot" in *The Red Wheel* (1984)

March 1917, Russian edition, 4 vols., the third "knot" in *The Red Wheel* (1986–88)

April 1917, Russian, edition, 2 vols., the fourth "knot" in *The Red Wheel* (1991)

What a Pity and Other Stories (1996)

November 1916 (1998)

POETRY

Prussian Nights (1977)

PLAYS

The Love Girl and the Innocent (1969)

Candle in the Wind (1976)

Victory Celebrations (1983)

Prisoners (1983)

MEMOIRS

Solzhenitsyn: A Pictorial Autobiography (1974)

The Oak and the Calf, Sketches of Literary Life in the Soviet Union (1980)

Invisible Allies (1995)

A Grain Landed Between Two Milestones: Essays from Exile, Russian edition (1996)

OTHER WORKS

The Voice of Freedom (1975)

A World Split Apart (1978)

Mortal Danger: How Misconceptions About Russia Imperil America (1981)

Rebuilding Russia (1991)

The Russian Question at the End of the Twentieth Century (1995)

Russia in Ruin (1998)

WORKS ABOUT ALEKSANDR SOLZHENITSYN AND HIS WRITINGS

Stephen Allaback, *Solzhenitsyn.* New York: Taplinger, 1978.

Dorothy Atkinson, "Solzhenitsyn's Heroes as Russian Historical Types," *Russian Review,* January 1971.

Francis Barker, *Solzhenitsyn: Politics and Form.* New York: Holmes and Meier, 1977.

Edward J. Brown, "Solzhenitsyn's Cast of Characters," *Slavic and East European Journal,* Spring 1971.

Stephen Carter, *The Politics of Solzhenitsyn.* London: Macmillan, 1977.

Olivier Clement, *The Spirit of Solzhenitsyn.* Trans. Sarah Fawcett and Paul Burns. London: Search, 1976.

Neil Cornwell, ed., *Reference Guide to Russian Literature.* London and Chicago: Fitzroy Dearborn, 1998.

James Curtis, *Solzhenitsyn's Traditional Imagination.* Athens: University of Georgia Press, 1984.

John B. Dunlop, Richard Haugh, and Alexis Klimoff, eds., *Aleksandr Solzhenitsyn: Critical Essays and Documentary Materials.* 2nd ed. New York and London: Collier Macmillan, 1975.

John B. Dunlop, Richard Haugh, and Michael Nicholson, eds., *Solzhenitsyn in Exile: Critical Essays and Documentary Materials.* Stanford, CA: Hoover Institution, 1985.

Edward E. Ericson, *Solzhenitsyn: The Moral Vision.* Grand Rapids, MI: Eerdmans, 1980.

Kathryn Feuer, ed., *Solzhenitsyn: A Collection of Critical Essays.* Englewood Cliffs, NJ: Prentice-Hall, 1976.

Michael Harris, "Solzhenitsyn's Russia on the Edge of Revolt," *Los Angeles Times,* May 10, 1999.

Andrej Kodjak, *Alexander Solzhenitsyn.* Boston: Twayne, 1978.

Vladislav Krasnov, *Solzhenitsyn and Dostoevsky: A Study in the Polyphonic Novel.* Athens: University of Georgia Press, 1980.

Leopold Labedz, ed., *Solzhenitsyn: A Documentary Record.* London: Allen Lane/Penguin, 1970.

Zhores A. Medvedev, *Ten Years After Ivan Denisovich.* Trans. Hillary Sternberg. New York: Alfred A. Knopf, 1973.

Christopher Moody, *Solzhenitsyn.* New York: Barnes and Noble, 1976.

Helen Muchnic, *Russian Writers: Notes and Essays.* New York: Random House, 1971.

Abraham Rothberg, *Aleksandr Solzhenitsyn: The Major Novels.* Ithaca, NY: Cornell University Press, 1971.

Leonid Rzhevsky, *Solzhenitsyn: Creator and Heroic Deed.* Trans. Sonja Miller. Tuscaloosa: University of Alabama Press, 1978.

Paul Siegel, *The Great Reversal: Politics and Art in Solzhenitsyn.* San Francisco: Walnut, 1991.

George Steiner, "In Exile Wherever He Goes," *New York Times Book Review,* March 1, 1998.

Carol J. Williams, "Solzhenitsyn's Latest Book Delights a Few, Bores Most," *Los Angeles Times*, June 5, 1998.

SOLZHENITSYN'S LIFE AND TIMES

David Burg and George Feifer, *Solzhenitsyn: A Biography.* New York: Stein and Day, 1972.

Olga Carlisle, S*ozhenitsyn and the Secret Circle.* New York: Holt, Rinehart and Winston, 1978.

Dorinda Elliott, "Solzhenitsyn Goes Home," *Newsweek,* June 6, 1994.

Max Hayward and Edward L. Crowley, eds., *Soviet Literature in the Sixties.* New York and London: Praeger, 1964.

Priscilla Johnson and Leopold Labedz, eds., *Khrushchev and the Arts.* Cambridge, MA: M.I.T. Press, 1965.

Fred Kaplan, "Solzhenitsyn's Journey Back," *Boston Globe,* May 22, 1994.

Greg Myre, "Aleksandr Solzhenitsyn Turns Eighty," *Associated Press,* December 11, 1998.

Michael Scammell, *Solzhenitsyn: A Biography.* New York: W.W. Norton, 1984.

D.M. Thomas, *A Century in His Life.* New York: St. Martin's, 1998.

WEBSITES

Freedom of Thought (www.fink.com/papers/freedom.html). Owned and maintained by Kevin Fink, the website offers an analysis of *One Day* in terms of existentialism.

Nobel Prize Internet Archive (www.almaz.com/nobel/Solzhenitsyn.html). Contains information on the works and lives of past winners of the Nobel Prize in literature, including Solzhenitsyn.

Overview of *One Day* (www.shs.springfield.k12.il.us/proj/aptheme/APThemesStudentProjs/SolzhenitsynOneDay/solzhenitsyndaymenu.htm). Maintained by the Springfield Public School District 186, the website offers an in-depth investigation of *One Day* and other major literary works. Analysis is provided by Advanced Placement Literature and Composition senior students.

Pleasures of the Mind: Aleksandr Solzhenitsyn (www.members.aol.com/KatharenaE/private/Alsolz.html). Maintained by Katharena Eiermann, this website offers several articles on Solzhenitsyn's life and works, including book reviews and many links.

Solzhenitsyn at Work (www.boston.com/globe/search/ stories/nobel/1984/1984ae.html). This website, maintained by the *Boston Globe*, offers various articles on Solzhenitsyn.

Solzhenitsyn's Autobiography (www.Nobel.sdsc.edu/ laureates/literature-1970-1-autobio.html). This site contains an autobiography and a photograph of Solzhenitsyn.

Solzhenitsyn's Biography (www.levity.com/corduroy/ solzheni.htm). Contains a short biography of Solzhenitsyn.

Teachers Guides (www.penguinputnam.com/guides/index. htm). Maintained by publisher Penguin Putnam, this website offers a comprehensive guide to *One Day* as well as a number of other classic and modern novels.

INDEX